Theology Today
39 Seeing and Believing:
   Theology and Art

Theology Today

GENERAL EDITOR:
EDWARD YARNOLD, S.J.

No. 39

Seeing and Believing
Theology and Art

BY

WILLIAM A. PURDY

distributed by
CLERGY BOOK SERVICE

BUTLER, WISCONSIN

204903

EPIGRAPH

An aged man is but a paltry thing,
A tattered coat upon a stick, unless
Soul clap its hands and sing, and louder sing
For every tatter in its mortal dress,
Nor is there singing school but studying
Monuments of its own magnificence.

Sailing to Byzantium
W.B. Yeats.

CONTENTS

ACKNOWLEDGEMENTS

The Scripture quotations in this publication are taken from the Revised Standard Version of the Bible, copyrighted © 1946 and 1952 by the Division of Christian Education of the National Council of the Churches of Christ in the USA and are used by kind permission. For other copyright material thanks are due to the following publishers: J Murray for the quotation from *Byzantine Aesthetics* by G Mathew; Thames and Hudson for the quotation from *Gothic Architecture and Scholasticism* by E Panofsky; Harvard University Press for the quotation from *Feast of Fools* by H Cox; and Rainbird Publishing Group for the quotation from *St Peter's* by J Lees-Milne.

FOREWORD

This book seeks to explore the connection between art and theology. It is not, however, an abstract study of the connection between aesthetics and grace, a theoretical Christian philosophy of man-made beauty. Most of its pages are devoted to a historical survey of Christians' attempts to embody their religious beliefs in works of art, especially the visual arts; but it is much more than a history of religious art. It is Mgr Purdy's aim to show how the developments in the religious art of every age reflect developments in religious thought. Gradually the author's deepest concern is revealed — to show that art is a parallel activity to theology, and not merely its 'visual aid'. Art and theology have the same goal: both are 'raids on the inarticulate', attempts to extend the basic experience of faith into new fields. The artist and the theologian both attempt to capture this experience, each in his own medium, and to communicate it to others.

The artist and the theologian need each other. The artist needs the theologian to check the exuberance of his vision and to rescue it from isolation and subjectivity by linking it with the consciousness of the Church. The theologian needs the artist to enrich his thinking and rescue it from aridity and irrelevance by linking it with the aspirations of humanity.

The liturgy exhibits the interdependence of the two activities. A liturgy that does not draw adequately upon the resources of art will not enter fully into men's lives; an aesthetically pleasing liturgy built on an inadequate theology will influence men's lives, but the influence will be unbalanced.

E. J. Yarnold, S.J.

1
INTRODUCTION

Why write about the relation of the arts to Christianity, or the Church, or theology, today? If the approach is merely a historical one the answer is easy enough. The art historian, whose discipline has flourished hugely in recent years, argues convincingly that both the quality of a work and its relevance to us can be better realised by knowing about the conditions, the ideas, the rules under which it was produced. It speaks a language we must learn before we can appreciate, criticize, respond to it as a work of art. Though this approach is not invulnerable to pedantry, jargon and mystification, the knowledge it gives can make much even of the most famous criticism of slightly earlier ages sound affected and jejune. Since religious themes or purposes so long dominated art in the past, a knowledge of Christian social history, philosophy, theology, devotional or mystical writing and of their inter-action with other kinds of knowledge, is indispensable to the serious art historian. Moreover all real knowledge involves some degree of sympathy.

Looking at the matter the other way round, the student of the history of Christian life and thought can learn a great deal more from works of architecture, sculpture and painting than for long he realised. Church historians have commonly been content with appending a brief chapter on the arts to their discussions of power-struggles and heresies; scholastic philosophers, horrified at leaving anything out, would have a brief note on "Beauty" in their manuals; theologians would be even more chary. Caution was not unwise, since it is better to ignore anything, however important, than to write about it from ignorance or from a wrong motive. There are greater pitfalls for the religious writer approaching works of art or periods of art history than for the art historian seeking enlightenment from Church history or theology. The former has a bias towards apologetics and edification which if not

11

controlled by scrupulous critical attention will betray him. It may lead him to mistake good intentions for talent, or religiosity for faith and insight. The churchman has a certain responsibility, which easily becomes an appetite, for making moral judgements. Even when judging men and events he may err by crudeness, narrowness, rashness. When he transfers his moral censorship to works of art his capacity for error multiplies, because here the equipment needed for a true judgement is wider and more various. He may strain at gnats while cheerfully swallowing what the instructed critic will see as camels.

This will not, I hope, be taken to mean that moral judgements have no place in criticism of works of art. But there is no moral judgement to be exercised in isolation from sensibility to the work of art. To think otherwise is the fallacy of censorship, one of whose dangers T. S. Eliot has pointed out (speaking of literature):

> . . . it gives people a false sense of security in leading them to believe that books which are *not* suppressed are harmless. Whether there *is* such a thing as a harmless book I am not sure; but there are very likely books so utterly unreadable as to be incapable of injuring anybody. But it is certain that a book is not harmless because no one is consciously offended by it.[1]

The moral censor of art, when he is not also aware of how a work of art functions, is in continual danger of preferring the vacuous because it is safe, or of overvaluing what is overtly edifying. This can be demonstrated from any period of history, but is more evident the less healthy the relationship between art and society. But can we in this age write about the relation of the arts to Christianity or to theology except as a matter of history? Has the theme any value except as a help to the art historian or the historian of Christianity? Is it likely to offer any help for living today?

So much of past history conditions us to consider the

---

(1) T.S. Eliot, *Selected Essays* (Faber & Faber 1932), pp. 393-4.

relation in only one way. For long ages such a high proportion of great buildings, statues, pictures were commissioned by or for the church and had religious themes or purposes that we can only think of the artist as either the servant of the Church or estranged from it. Some even see the estrangement as the proper natural state — a liberation which has been slowly and hardly won. Religious art has been arguably moribund for two centuries — not indeed a high proportion of human history — and some would see this as a symptom of our decline, others as an important example of modern emancipation. But are servitude or estrangement the only possible relationships? Both history and present experience suggest that the question is worthy of investigation.

Some considerable attention to history is necessary to achieve an accurate perspective of the often complex and shifting relations of art and Christian society even when these were broadly based and taken for granted. Each of the 'historic styles' looked at in the succeeding chapters presents a different pattern of relationships, involving most often a building, its decoration, images, the Church whether considered as a community, a teacher, a patron, an inspirer of artists or a promoter of public or private patronage — patronage which in its turn may set up complex relations between belief, devotion, patriotism or civic pride, family pride or desire to perpetuate remembrance. The effect of the multiplication of museums — a relatively modern development — was to divest works of art of their function and much of their significance and to present them crowded together in the least digestible state, though in some countries at least enough works remained *in situ* and even fulfilled their intended functions to give the serious inquirer a start towards understanding them. But no more than a start. The modern man standing in a Byzantine, romanesque, gothic or baroque church might not only have lost touch with the ideas, feelings, motives, way of life, social relationships of those by and for whom it was built; he might also have interposed theories, sentiments, beliefs of his own (romantic, neo-classical, marxist or whatever) which acted as veils between him and what he was looking at.

Serious art history obviously diminishes the first handicap; obliquely it diminishes the second, since the more we know about a thing the less likely we are to fasten our own theories on it and weave our own fancies about it. Serious art history then and consequently criticism can benefit from knowing more about Christian belief and life. Conversely theology and allied disciplines improve their method when they widen their view by a proper estimate of works of art as theological *loci*. In the past theology has often seemed to walk in blinkers, confining itself to the scrutiny of a few conventional sources. To put it another way, it has often seemed content to nourish itself on a limited and monotonous diet. But if theologians approach works of art as quarries which can yield something useful apart from their existence and quality as works of art they are not likely to take away anything of much value, not likely to improve their diet.

Art is not, whatever churchmen may at times have thought, primarily one human activity at the service of another — though to say this is not another way of subscribing to the doctrine of 'art for art's sake'. A work of art may witness to the faith of a people and an age — to its 'knowledge of Christ, the question and the answer' which is its theology. A work of art may also influence the formulation of faith and religious sentiment. But it will only do so seriously *as* a work of art. The artist, 'the poet's eye in a fine frenzy rolling', ranges wide even over a religious subject. Equally, he may betray a religious concern in the most unlikely place; but he will not betray it to anyone, theologian or not, who does not know how to look at or listen to a work of art. The artist's *discipline* is of another kind from the theologian's but is no less strict and may be much stricter. Art sings the glory of God in its own way (whether deliberately or unconsciously and involuntarily) and only by learning patiently what that way is shall we respond to the work truly. This is as true of works of plastic art which were produced under strict surveillance and patronage or iconographical or other rules, like Byzantine mosaics or gothic building or statuary, as of works like Shakespeare's plays, products and symptoms of a society in transition. Here the religious notes, being hardly ever explicit, but depending on an understanding of association, of the interplay of imagery, of relations of words much wider than that of the immediate context, have to be sensitively listened for and never isolated from the totality of the poem.

An apologetical approach to works of art, picking about among them for signs or hints of a religious concern or support for a theological point, is the kiss of death, but this is not to say that a work of art which has no explicit religious theme or material is of no religious interest.

I have concerned myself principally with the figurative arts — which alone, except for music, seem to exemplify the commonplace that art knows no frontiers. To respond properly to a great work of art we must learn the language in which it is written. Where the spoken word is involved this is, sometimes at least, quite evident — the translation of a great poem into another language is generally the most useless exercise, or at best can serve secondary purposes. But it is easy and dangerous to forget that the 'language' of a picture or a statue or a church or a setting of the mass, while transcending perhaps* geography or language barriers in the literal sense, may be double dutch to the uninstructed, though much less obviously.

Churchmen have often been loathe to concede this, even in the ages when Church patronage still dominated or played a large part in the figurative arts. Today when religious art (though showing I believe more signs of health than it did) is a minor activity and usually no more easily accessible to the layman's understanding than any other contemporary art, we ought logically to be less tempted to presumption. But a depressingly high proportion of churchmen fall into one of two classes: either they dismiss a work as irrelevant to their concerns because it fails to answer to some historically-

---

* perhaps — not always, as witness the failure of the Italians to master gothic architectural language, or the rarity with which they perform Bach with any success.

conditioned requirement of their own, or else they are 'trendy' and prepared to give ecclesiastical hospitality to anything fashionable, mystifying or bizarre.

Trendiness and dull conservatism are twin products of an ailing society and neither of them represent a proper relationship between the artist and the serious Christian. A proper relationship, it seems to me should not take its beginning from either satisfaction or lamentation that the world which produced Ravenna or Rheims or San Biagio or Die Wies or Palestrina or Bach is dead. Serious artists have (as they always have had) this in common with serious Christians and indeed with serious humanists — that they take man seriously and from this it is a short, natural step to taking the world, one might even say the earth, seriously. (Hopkins is a ready recent example of the link between the two and his poetry is profoundly human and religious together.) The artist's affinity is perhaps more with the saint, the prophet, the mystic* or, as it seems we must now inevitably say, the charismatic than with the theologian, but the common concern for man embraces them all. When man is more and more exploited and manipulated, when his life is held cheap and the means of destroying it are highly sophisticated, when even the environment in which he must live and breathe is despised, polluted, destroyed, he should be deeply interested in two callings (not the only two) which have a long history of reverence for man, of ambition to expand his horizons, raise him up, liberate his spirit, intensify his vision, beautify his surroundings, admit him both to ecstasy and to divine discontent. For the artist and for the theologian, we may be good or bad but we are not junk.

---

* ". . . though in a wholly different order, the universe of the artist resembles that of the contemplative. In this, the contemplative's world, said Pascal, everything is hiding a mystery; in the artist's, the thing hidden is not God, but everything is the sign of something else. . . . It is not to be wondered at that every masterpiece should have a quality of mystery, for it really is the revelation of a mystery."
E.Gilson *Choir of Muses*
Sheed & Ward London 1953, pp184-5

The function of patron, of provider of programmes is now and probably will remain a minor part of the churchman's relationship with the artist, though there is no reason why it should shrink further rather than expand. To suppose that the church will maintain any connection with the artist merely by developing the alternative function of external moral censor of works whose language the theologian takes no trouble to learn, is an illusion long exploded. It seems that hope lies rather in the churchman standing together with the artist in the rebellion against pretentiousness, shoddy work, cosy mediocrity, escapism, and against the contempt for man's intelligence and feelings that goes with it. The air of manipulation and exploitation, of violence to human sensibility is not an air in which men more readily hold to Christ and grow in his knowledge.

It is easy to point to periods of history from which there is ample surviving evidence that the Church was aware of this, took it for granted almost. But today, when the awareness is more necessary than ever it was, signs of it are fitful. To judge by the jumble of things ranging from masterpieces to intolerable rubbish that find places, sometimes side by side, on church walls or in niches, in prayer books and hymnals or other religious literature, the churchman, whatever his concern for the message of salvation, is little concerned about who he is delivering it to and in what kind of wrapping. If this is so we cannot complain if people become unconcerned about us and our message. Unless we are the plainest of fundamentalists — perhaps even if we are — there is something to think about here both historically and in relation to our own time.

The last chapter of this book is really a continuation of the first. The intervening chapters are not a potted history of art. They are an attempt to illustrate, with reference to works I am more or less familiar with (I have avoided writing about things I have not seen except in the case of Dura Europos and the Syrian churches) the proposition (page 131) that each of the historical styles presents a different pattern of relationships between Church, artist and work of art; yet a survey of the succession of patterns yields much that is helpful for making the most important judgements, which are those about the present situation. This implies no advocacy of a return to past relationships, still less a return to past styles. The most slavish imitation of earlier styles has generally gone with very limited knowledge of what those styles intended to do or say. On the other hand, I accept the main principles set out by Eliot (himself a powerful innovator enough) on the relations of "Tradition and the Individual Talent". I content myself with quoting the principle he explicitly extends beyond poetry to all the arts:

> No poet, no artist of any art, has his complete meaning alone. His significance, his appreciation is the appreciation of his relation to the dead poets and artists. You cannot value him alone; you must set him, for contrast and comparison, among the dead. I mean this as a principle of aesthetic, not merely historical, criticism.

It seems to me at least equally a principle for the kind of assessment of relationships between Church, theologian, artist and work of art to which I am tentatively pointing here.

2
ORIGINS

It has been said that Christian art was 'born old'. This is true in the sense that the first Christians, possessed by a faith which they had little time, opportunity or command of skill to express in artistic work, borrowed the conventions of the time in their more modest forms. In art they were the heirs of old, rich and complex traditions, but among such heirs they were for a time the poor relations. The caveman, drawing beautifully under possibly religious impulses which we can only guess at, was a primitive; the man drawing on catacomb walls or carrying out an order for a sarcophagus was derivative in terms of art, but expressing in his generally clumsy, eclectic way something which theologically was at once profoundly new and rooted in the ancient tradition of the bible.

The latter in its turn was linked by many ties with the ancient civilisations of the near east. It too was a poor relation (materially at least) of the great theocratic city-states of antiquity.

That great primary source for Christian theology, the Bible, may be considered for our purposes in three ways: as a locus for Jewish and Christian attitudes to art, as itself containing works of art (a good deal of the force of which will have been lost in translation)[1] and as an inspiration to artists.

Genesis 3-9 tells of men making bricks and setting out to build a city and 'a tower with its top in the heavens' We are here at one of the sources of our civilisation, the region of the lower Tigris and Euphrates, one of the two river valley regions (the other lies beyond the Arabian desert and Mt Sinai, in the valley of the Nile) where the prodigies of archaeology have

---

(1) I am not forgetting that a great translation may be a work of art in itself and have a wide, deep and prolonged influence. But it is not the influence of the original *work of art*.

revealed a buried world of cities in which picture-writing and religion go hand in hand from the first.

Lacking revelation, men make themselves gods after the fashion of their needs. The mother goddess was first the virgin huntress and mistress of the beasts, but at the dawn of history she is the goddess of the fertile fields, the mistress of the harvest. The Sumerian years and worship are bound up with the seasons — the recurrence of birth and death in nature; they celebrate the divine marriage, the wedding of God and they lament his death, the widowing of the mother goddess. This archaic culture is founded on the god's temple and its estate and architecture and allied arts were as inseparable from religion as were the activities of everyday life, or political authority. The king was a priest-king ruling in place of the God, the temple was church, centre of learning and economy, storehouse and bank. Artists lavished their skill on it, governed by rigid traditions but patronised and stimulated by wealthy, leisured patrons.

Building materials were limited. Gudea of Lagash made the first brick for his temple in a consecrated mould as a model, and a well-shaped brick (often richly revetted) was to remain a medium of good building for many centuries. The tower of Babel was a ziggurat, a stepped, mountain-like structure with the shrine on top. It had a crude theological idea behind it — that thus the god could more easily descend to his earthly shrine. But the Genesis narrative sees it as a symbol of heathen pride which God thwarts and punishes. It was away from all this that he led Abraham into the promised land. Perhaps thus early we have the seeds of an ambiguity in the attitude of the People of God: the principle that nothing but the best is good enough for the Lord is open to a vulgar, newly-rich interpretation which a reaction then sees as heathen vanity. Luxury had an immemorial association with idols.

Egypt, to which Abraham and his followers went to escape famine, and with which the chosen people were to be long associated, was another land with a life and art immemorially dominated by absolute theocracy; artistic conventions fixed in the fifth dynasty (years before Joseph went there) never greatly altered. A religious state-socialism put vast resources, including slave-labour, behind the building and decorating of the temples over several millennia. A confusing pantheon of deities half-human, half-animal with complicated ritual provided plentiful subject-matter; pylons, columns, vast wall-space gave scope to painter and sculptor. The Egyptian attitude to death (they disliked thinking of people as dead at all and preferred to think of the tomb as a make-believe temporary lodging) produced the pyramids and the mastabas as well as portraiture and bric-a-brac. But the art was as static as the religion it expressed (only one pharoah, Tutankhamen's predecessor Iknahton, tried vainly to break out of the tyranny of the ancient, all-devouring ritual and artistic conventions), and 'when Israel went forth from Egypt, the house of Jacob from a people of strange language' (Ps 113.1), there must have been boredom as well as revulsion recollected in the poet's contrast: 'Our god is in the heavens, he does whatever he pleases. Their idols are silver and gold, the work of men's hands. They have mouths but do not speak, eyes but do not see', and in the scornful conclusion 'Those who make them are like them; so are all who trust in them' (cf. Deut 4. 27 ff.; 29.17; Ex 20.11).

The decalogue began by solemnly forbidding the making and worship of idols, and whether or not the Book of the Covenant (Deut 20.23) forbids the making of images of Yahweh, it is certain that image-making was not absolutely forbidden from the fact that the cover of the Ark, the propitiatory, was mounted by two gold cherubim with outspread wings. An Egyptian ark at Dendera has similar figures and this is only one indication that the style and materials that went into the portable tabernacle, the Ark and other ritual furnishing derived from Egypt, like the skill of Bezalel and Ohotrab who worked them, though the Lord had called these men and endowed them with their gifts (Ex 35.30,31). A people liable to lapse into the idolatrous ways of more powerful neighbours were even more susceptible to their ancient and rich artistic traditions.

An excess of free-will offerings, which had to be restrained, provided the materials. The prefabricated and portable shrine was thoroughly sumptuous. It provided the basic plan for the future temple. The tabernacle, divided into Holy of Holies, the *naos* where the Ark rested, and the Holy Place, was enclosed in a 'forecourt' of hangings, and in front of it was an altar (very simple, of earth or uncut stone as directed — Ex 20.24-6). On the rail surrounding the altar there were even projections to be grasped by those taking sanctuary. The functions of the divisions were clear: God dwelt in the Holy of Holies, gave audience to his ministers in the Holy Place and received the homage of his people in the forecourt.

1 Kings 5, describes how Solomon (c 972-931) at last felt able to build a permanent sanctuary and enlisted the help of Hiram of Tyre, who supplied cedars of Lebanon, men who could cut them and a master workman, Huramabi. The building and furnishings are described in careful detail in the next two chapters and in 2 Chron 3 and 4. The fine rock platform site on Mount Moriah was a conventional choice. What strikes us is the care about good and fit materials and workmanship rather than any originality; though reconstructions depend largely on the sparse pagan analogies that archaeology offers. (The measurements given in 1 Kings 6.2 suggest a building about the size of the Sainte Chapelle in Paris or the Theseion at Athens.) For long the best parallel was (in spite of its very different spirit and age) the Ionic temple, but discoveries at Tel Tainab in 1936 linked Solomon's temple with the Syrian Iron Age.

Reading of the building of Solomon's palace in 3 Kings 7 is like listening to a rich bore, and the details of the building of the temple might sound little different were they not sublimated by the noble speech and prayer (7.12-61, cf. 2 Chron 6) breathing the spirit of the covenant and of Israel's sense of vocation and mission. Crude as the sacrificial cult was, this was really the house of the Lord, and of his glory, whose beauty the psalmist loved.

This was the temple first partially despoiled (597) and then destroyed (587) by Nabuchodonosor (4 Kings 24.13; 25.9 ff.).

It was to raise the morale of the Babylonian exiles that

Ezekiel gave his visionary description of the new Jerusalem with its temple and cult (Ez 40-48). Though the building was not specially original and in some details unrealisable, nothing conveys more vividly what sacred art meant to the Jews — what was the symbolic and emotive force of the conception of the house of God, whom the prophet sees solemnly entering by the eastern gate and promising to dwell forever among his people (43.1-12).

Rebuilding of the temple began in 520, 17 years after the return from exile, under the inspiration of the prophets Haggai and Zechariah. It was dedicated in 516, the same year as the Doric temple of Apollo at Delphi, and it stood, though often menaced and profaned, until almost the beginning of the Christian era, 20-19 B.C., when Herod planned his new temple (that of the gospels) to be finished only six years before the fall of Jerusalem to Titus.

By the time Christians came to build and donate churches they were dependent on the literary sources for their knowledge of temples built, in accordance with Yahweh's commands, by his chosen people. Though the themes of their painting and sculpture had, as we shall see, long drawn on Old Testament material, they derived little from the tradition of the tabernacle and the temple except the leading idea of making the house of God worthy. The idea was put into practice in the style of the society to which they belonged — cosmopolitan Rome, whose dependence on Hellenic models was by that time already much modified by oriental influences.

But all this is post-Constantinian. If, before Constantine, there were above-ground Christian buildings distinctively for worship we know very little about them. The origins of Christian art must be sought elsewhere.

Christian catacombs with painted decorations and incised or carved tomb-slabs (very few *in situ*) are to be found in the East and in Italy and Provence. They developed out of small family vaults. None can be traced with certainty before the end of the second century and only about eleven are pre-Constantinian. Not surprisingly they reveal little originality or virtuosity as works of art; but their interest to the theologian is greater than he always appreciates. They may be formally funerary art, but they are concerned with Christian life. When this art appears in the baptistery of a domestic chapel at Dura it is theologically more aptly housed.

The beginning of Christian art may coincide with the tolerance shown by the Severan emperors. The same applies to Jewish art, which we first meet alongside Christian and pagan art in the houses of Dura, the little provincial Roman town on the Euphrates. The superior pagan work there, of a type which may later have influenced Byzantine art, goes back to A.D. 85, but the Jewish and Christian work only to 245 and 250. Both indicate that by this time the Jewish dislike (no doubt originally shared by Christians) of religious portraiture had given way under Hellenistic influence. Old Testament scenes naturally are treated much alike by the two, though Jewish work is better.

Pagan motives as well as style and design are to be found in the earliest catacomb paintings (St Domitilla and the crypt of Lucina). Parallels with such things as the 'Neo-Pythagorean' underground temple at Porta Maggiore are commonplace. Of more interest here is the distinctively Christian element, often veiled and symbolic.

The New Testament says little or nothing about art. The apostles encountered it in idolatrous cities. When Paul was at Athens 'his spirit was provoked within him when he saw that the city was full of idols' (Acts 17.16). The Athenians thought him a babbler of strange things, but some were impressed by his tactful speech about the unknown God and his quoting their poets. 'Being then God's offspring we ought not to think that the deity is like gold or silver or stone, a representation by the art and imagination of man. The times of ignorance God overlooked, but now he commands all men to repent. . . .' (Acts 17.29-30). It was bold stuff to talk to the Athenians, whose dignified though politically decayed city was the heart of Greek religion, a religion supremely anthropomorphic and art-expressed. Even the cult of athletics which produced so many great Greek statues was basically religious. But the art, even at its least impressive, was greater than the theology behind it. In the age of Marathon, Salamis and Plataea, the belief that a small state favoured by the gods had vanquished numbers and wealth had an impressiveness not unlike that of Israel, and 'the exaltation that ensued bred great designs'. But the Greeks saw the gods as supreme embodiments of power and immortality, not of mystery and love. 'It would be eccentric for anyone to say that he loved Zeus', said one of Aristotle's followers. The religion of Athens was already being questioned in the days of Pericles. Anaxagoras the cosmologist, Euripides the dramatist, Thucydides the historian were all 'heretics'. Plato, suspicious and conservative about the arts, condemned the artistic manifestations of the same questioning spirit — the sensual, violent, rhetorical Hellenistic works culminating in the Laocoon, where art is becoming not only an end in itself but a criticism of religion. (Laocoon is a Trojan priest savagely destroyed with his children by the Olympian gods because he has stood in the way of their designs). The restlessness and nervous energy of much Hellenistic sculpture reflects the complex spiritual forces that were agitating the no less complex world that Alexander and then the power of Rome had made possible. The refining process by which the Greeks came to represent their gods in the forms of physical beauty and perfect manhood had its limits and led at last to monotony and rebellion. (Christian art was later to relearn the same lesson).

Still, we should not belittle the Greek achievement, so warm, so colourful, so exhilarating in its marvellous Mediterranean setting, so ill-commemorated in the cold marbles of our dull museums. Paul's words to the Athenians are perhaps more than apologetical tact — they hint at some reverence for a great past.

At Ephesus it was different. The huge Artemision, shrine of the ancient mother-goddess (today a few sad, half-drowned fragments), with its revolting many-breasted cult statue, was reproduced in silver models to be sold to the devout, much as gilded, battery-lighted models of St Peter's are sold in Rome today. The Greek spirit had far declined. Paul's preaching, 'gods made with hands are not gods' (Acts 19.26) threatened a vested interest. The reaction was hysteria, which only the good sense of the town clerk quieted. It was no wonder that the first Christian steps in art were tentative.

Yet the heart of the matter was there, in the gospels. The heart of the mystery was 'the Word was made flesh and dwelt amongst us'. The creed commits us to great mysteries but also to historical events, or rather to the mysteries through the events. Zeus took on human form to play unprepossessing tricks; the Son of God emptied himself, taking the form of a servant, to save all men. But the Incarnation would allow us in the end to take up the classical inheritance fully.

Meantime it is there, inescapable, in the first gropings of the catacombs. The truth that the Church learned to express her thought about Christ rather as a child learns from contact with other minds, debate within the Church and with pagans gradually sharpening the concepts used,[2] can be verified also in Christian art. It takes up first the themes of Christian initiation, the gospel sacraments. The pre-Constantinian Christians were in no danger of seeing the Church chiefly as the institution, blotting out the sacrament of salvation. To be a Christian was to be delivered into 'a place of refreshment, light and peace'. It was baptism and the Eucharist rather than death that did this; hence the themes of cemetery paintings and sarcophagus carvings were the gospel sacraments and their Old Testament paradigms. The pathos of the pagan funeral feast, expressed e.g. in the memorial slab of Aelia Secundula in the cemetery on the Via Nomentana, merged into the Christian memoria, which was an assertion of life.

In the oldest catacomb-paintings in the crypt of Lucina, the baptizer helps the candidate up from the water, and the dove hovers, the seal of the Spirit. But more often, Old Testament scenes, the story of Jonah with its three episodes, Moses striking the rock, the deliverance of Daniel, Susanna and the three youths in the furnace (the themes of the readings of the one-

---

(2) cf. Ralph Woodhall, S.J., *The Theology of the Incarnation*, Mercier Press.

time Easter vigil prophecies), figure the deliverance of baptism. So do the New Testament scenes of the healed paralytic and the women at the well, or simply the symbols of the fish and the anchor and the figure of the divine Fisherman and the Shepherd. The Christian sarcophagus of Brignolles, made at Arles and probably the oldest surviving, is not overcrowded and clearly shows in a row, the Sun, the fisherman, the *orans* in a paradise indicated by a bird in a tree, the Teacher and the Shepherd — all motives to be linked with baptism.

We shall return to these, but first the Eucharist must be considered. It is seen, not without ambiguities, within the broader concept of *refrigerium*, which includes food, drink and even shade as in the popular scene of Jonah resting under the gourd. There is no space to discuss the degrees of explicit reference to the Eucharist in the numerous and varied banquet scenes (which were a convention of pagan funerary art), but one of the earliest eucharistic pictures is also one of the clearest — in the crypt of Lucina, a basket of loaves against which is a wine vessel, both resting on a fish. Seeing this as early evidence of reservation, S.G.A. Luff quotes a passage from St Jerome, Letter 125.[3] Sometimes, as on the Baebia Herofile sarcophagus or in the chapel of the sacraments at S Callisto, the eucharistic reference of a banquet is clear from the surrounding pictures.

The history of the representation of Christ is theologically interesting. It seems clear that for long it was not done at all; then, if not 'secretively', at least in a veiled, symbolic way. Both the early examples I have used above have the figure of the shepherd, youthful and beardless, an ancient pagan motif very convenient to adapt in view of Christ's words (John 10.11-16), surrounded by his flock in the paradise-gardens, carrying his milk pail, associated with the *orans*, i.e. the praying church or the delivered soul; or even quite cheerfully with pagan subjects, a bacchic vintage or Eros or Psyche, or the seasons. The figure became a cliche used on many objects and in many media.

---

(3) cf. Clergy Review, Vol. LVII (April, 1972), p.283.

A different conception derived from the more intellectual and 'apologetical' climate of Alexandria, that of Christ the teacher, the late classical philosopher, still beardless, with his academic robe and scroll, who taught True Wisdom; but it became equally popular and was destined to last much longer.

Clement of Alexandria held austere views about Christian iconography, contrasting with his more liberal views about the possibilities of philosophy (4. *Paed* III. 11, 59:2); and certainly, apart from actual heterodox work like that of the Aurelii tombs, pagan and Christian themes mingled pretty freely, side by side or even in the same work. That this was not dictated by any need for concealment is clear from the fact that it continued long after the Constantinian peace. The famous words *instinctu divinitatis* on the arch of Constantine are themselves an instance of the ambiguity. On the vault of what was probably his granddaughter's mausoleum (324-6) (later a baptistery and now the church of S Costanza) there are decidedly Roman mosaics whose gay vintage scenes and profusion of flowers and birds have no Christian tones, unless we count the symbolism of peacocks or grapes. The mosaics in the dome, however, known only from drawings, did contain Old Testament scenes, not all of the 'deliverance' repertoire, but there was also a rather frivolous Nile scene surrounding the base. Artistically of course this work is vastly superior to anything so far discussed, but in translating Christian sensibility, let alone theology, into plastic terms, it shows no progress — rather recession. The same may be said of the immensely lively and attractive mosaic floor of the same period at Aquileia where everything to do with water and fish (and hence baptism) is gaily crammed in (as well as a good shepherd and a possible eucharistic motive). There is work of similar interest at Centcelles, near Tarragona.

Of course Constantine's great contribution was his church-building — an empire-wide campaign which had an immense influence on the developments to be discussed in the next chapter. Their decoration may have begun these developments — we know practically nothing about it, but fourth-century developments in catacomb art, especially at SS Pietro and

Marcellino, probably reflect the mosaics of Rome's Constantinian churches (e.g. a bearded Christ between tall, grave apostles).

There is a great expansion of biblical themes in fourth-century sarcophagi, including scenes from Christ's life, showing him still as a beardless youth, while the introduction of architectural motives reflects the wider horizons of the freed Church. Catacomb-painting too is more ambitious, though the recent discoveries on the Via Latina show Christian funerary art still dominated by the Old Testament and. Christians content to share *hypogea* with Jews and pagans. These paintings belong to a tradition which was probably much more prolific in other fields now lost — manuscript-illumination, for example. Whether it corresponded to a much richer development of typology by theologians is now very hard to say.

There is a good deal in the scriptures and in the Christian tradition about the gentleness of the action of the Spirit. Perhaps it is better reflected in this first phase of Christian art than in, say, the fiery rhetoric of Tertullian. The need for unobtrusiveness combined with the problem of expressing the inexpressible and with submersion in old and deep artistic traditions to make the artistic witness a subdued one, economic of means. It was not often great art, but perhaps involuntarily it worked as great art does. Art that bludgeons our sensibilities and screams at us is bad art. Christian art got off to a good start in this sense, catching the spirit of the parables, whose theme is the 'pluralism' of the human situation. Perhaps today (as will be suggested later) we are recapturing something of this.

'Hold to Christ and for the rest be uncommitted'; the words are Herbert Butterfield's, but they express the spirit in which Christian art began.

THE IMPERIAL THEME

Since our earliest surviving Christian images post-date the crises of faith about Christ's genuine humanity (Docetism and some forms of Gnosticism) it is not easy to assess what was the impact of the latter on Christian art. The disciples could never see the footprints of Christ, said the Acts of John, because he walked on air. 'If these things were done by Our Lord in appearance only, then my bonds are a matter of appearance', retorted Ignatius of Antioch, writing to the Church of Smyrna. But the implications of Christ's 'perfect manhood' still awaited precise working out; and even if Christ was perfect man it remained true that to represent him as such, especially in the round, uncomfortably summoned up the idols housed in the classical temples. An unobtrusive relief of a bucolic shepherd-figure (an age-old convention with a new feeling) alluding to a psalm and a gospel passage, was in several ways safer. So was the figure, no less conventional though deriving from and appealing to quite different milieux, of the true teacher of wisdom.

Already about A.D. 200 Tertullian had objected to the shepherd-image stamped on chalices, and the objection was to recur, but went generally with puritan lack of moderation. The images remained, and with the enlarged freedom and imperial patronage of the fourth century, their scope expanded, though the old ambiguities did not disappear and new ones arose out of the new situation.

In the necropolis under St Peter's there is a mosaic, seemingly from the time of Constantine, showing a god-like figure, its head surrounded by sun-rays, mounting the sky in a chariot, the whole wreathed with vines. We are reminded of Dunbar's lines:

> The Cleir Sone, quhom no cloud devouris,
> Surmounting Phebus in the Est,
> Is cumin of his hevinly touris:
> *Et nobis Puer natus est.*

The image remains an isolated one in Christian art, but it points to modifications of Christian sensibility which, however slowly they spread, were crucial.

Enough has been written of the ambiguous character of imperial patronage for Christianity, of the deceptive ease of the transition from solar monotheism, of the dangers of imperial munificence and episcopal complaisance. History is a corrective to the simplicities and legends on which the imperial theme first rested. We are concerned here only with how the changes were reflected in the relations of theology and the arts.

It would be possible to make a selection of works suggesting little shift of interest, for the fourth century at least. The funerary art (which has best survived) multiplied its explicit biblical themes, including the Passion, but Christ's death is never portrayed. The shepherd gradually disappears, the youthful teacher assumes a late classical majesty as in the Vatican sarcophagus of the convert prefect Junius Bassus — though this is a rare instance where the quality of work rises about the low level of the arch of Constantine reliefs.

The great basilicas of Constantine have become a legend, and we easily forget how little we know of them directly. The best remains of the first great burst of Christian church-building, in the fourth century, are the ruins in Syria, destroyed by Islam and never restored. In Rome much more secular building has survived and it was more massive and grandiose than the churches, e.g. the basilica of Maxentius, finished by Constantine. Many statues of these fourth-century emperors remain, like the colossus on the Capitol, generally considered to be Constantine. The huge head with its bold staring eyes and hard mouth remind us that the man who put the Cross on his standard was the heir of a line of deified emperors and a very tough wielder of power.

We may remember too that Seneca had said, 'They pray and sacrifice before the images of the gods, but they despise the sculptor who made them.' This sculpture is bad art serving a curious theology in which *imperium* and *sacerdotium* are invested in one man, who may have come by bloodshed and indirection to represent God on earth, and be the arbiter of doctrinal disputes. By the next century, with the statue of Marcian[1] — still standing in the open street in Barletta — we are reminded of vulgar modern dictators. It is almost possible to sympathise with the pagan conservatives who saw no more in Christianity than this, with bishops preening themselves on ancient titles and insignia, and tax-exemptions inducing conversion.

It is not so simple of course. The portrait of Theodosius on an ornamental shield in Madrid, if it suggests a mystique of monarchy reinforced from Persia propped up by a powerful, classically educated bureaucracy, suggests also the better side of the imperial religion. Looking at the sensitive face rather than the halo and the *chlamys*, we can believe in the penance after the Thessalonian massacre, in the praise of Augustine, who did not write the *City of God* to praise emperors, and the lines of the stern Ambrose come back, almost as some of Virgil's lines do:

> *Si respicis labes cadunt*
> *Fletuque culpa solvitur.*

Constantine's vigorous building-campaign provided variations (as wide almost as the empire) on the theme of the 'basilica'. Because of the vast influence this type of church was to have on future Christian architecture, scholars have wrangled interminably about its genesis, mainly because they are juggling with very inadequate evidence. The three- or, in grand instances, five-aisled pillared oblong hall, with or without apse or rudimentary transept, sometimes preceded by a handsome *atrium* (Mosques give the best idea of this last effect now, though the new St Paul's in Rome offers it in a museum-like way) was a flexible type within which local variations, often reflecting local civic styles as in Syria, flourished. The only Constantinian example that perhaps survives more or less as it was is the Nativity church in Bethlehem.

The imperial fondness for imposing mausolea, traditionally

---

(1) Or Valentinian I

round, and the convenience of the same plan for baptisteries, established the lesser, parallel tradition of the rotunda. These two conceptions, sometimes combined, lie behind the whole immensely rich and varied Christian architectural development from the simple village church to the subtleties of space and volume, of flow and rest, in S Vitale or Vierzehnheiligen.

To the theologian, immediate interest lies in the building as a setting for worship. Christians first worshipped in rooms lent in private houses, then in houses given and roughly adapted as churches (like Dura), long before Constantine's churches were built, but we know hardly anything of them. In these early places the gospel sacraments and the ministry of the word governed all. Small assemblies allowed involvement, centred round the altar, with bishop seated on his throne, flanked by his presbyters. With this intimacy went great awe and reverence for the Eucharist, though it was treated more freely — received in the hand and even taken home.

The fourth century was a time of rapid evolution. Congregation and churches grew rapidly in size; the liturgy and its setting grew more elaborate and rich; the balance of awe over intimacy increased; the custom of screening off the eucharistic table, first by curtains then by an *iconostasis*, increased. But the pace for liturgical change was set in the East. A glance at a map for any time before Constantine will show a vastly greater concentration of churches in the eastern mediterranean (and latterly in North Africa) than in western Europe. The move to the Bosphorus merely gave wider scope to the richer originality and cultural variety of these churches, though it was long before New Rome ousted the old as 'The City'. The entrance of the imperial theme into Christian art went with the slow but steady increase of these complex influences, which yet never swamped the classical heritage.

With little surviving church-decoration, sarcophagi, reliquaries and diptychs show the imperial evolution in portraying Christ. The simple boy-shepherd gives way to a figure still at first youthful but now enthroned in majesty, surrounded by apostles, backed by the architecture of the celestial city, feet clasped by suppliants or planted on the orb of the world, giving the law to St Peter or St Paul. The shepherd makes a last appearance in the magical mausoleum of Galla Placidia at Ravenna, where the ripeness of Christian antiquity is already fused with Byzantium. Long before this another type has appeared (S Pudenziana or Naples baptistery — both about A.D. 400) the dark-haired, deep-eyed, bearded semitic figure which was to become the awesome *Pantocrator* of developed Byzantine art.

There is little or no reflection in fourth century art of the doctrinal and political struggles of that time. In the west the explanation is not hard to find — Hilary of Poitiers, for example, admitted he had been a bishop for years without hearing of the Nicene Creed, while even in the East the issues, though far from being mere wars of words, were not easily expressible in artistic terms. The 'Theodosian renaissance' in art took place in a world where Arianism was dead except among the Goths. What art reveals more clearly, especially in its more domestic forms, is the slowness of paganism to perish and of Christianity, even under the sometimes rather slapdash official patronage, to develop an assured idiom. Doubts about the whole enterprise had not been abandoned, as witness the famous story of the high-handed puritanical Cypriot bishop Epiphanius (d. 403), who, travelling in Palestine, torn down church-curtains decorated with pictures of Christ and saints.

The Nestorian dispute of the next century and the Council of Ephesus (431) had more far-reaching repercussions. The proclamation of the dogma of the *Theotokos* was strongly reflected in the decoration of the rebuilt St Mary Major in Rome. The city had been sacked by Alaric the Goth in 410, but, though the literary sources suggest this was a soul-searching experience, arousing the laments of Jerome and the questionings of Augustine in the *City of God* (neither of whom were writing on the spot), it left little lasting material effect on the city and hardly halted creative activity. The panels of the nave of the new church present Old Testament episodes in a rather old-fashioned style, but the revetment of the triumphal arch, besides illustrations of apocryphal writings designed to stress the maternal theme, has an 'Annunciation' and a 'Presentation'. In these biblical scenes (destined to become stock-in-trade) Our Lady is a queen, in the first spinning imperial purple in the temple, in the second carrying the divine Infant. The apse-mosaic belongs to a thirteenth-century rebuilding, but may follow the general theme of the original and shows its later development, with Christ placing the crown on his mother's head. In the East, Mary became a nun-like figure enveloped in dark blue, similar to the 'Church' personifications in S Sabina, and returns thus to influence the medieval West.

It is time to say something of the art stimulated by the cult of saints. This expanded enormously after 313, when *memoriae* (or *martyria* in the East) multiplied. Some of the imperial basilicas were *cemeteriales*, like Constantine's St Peter's itself, and Theodosius' St Paul's (a tragic nineteenth century loss). The cult of the martyrs' relics of course long pre-dated Constantine — the main Roman one, that of SS Peter and Paul, was on the Appia, *ad catacumbas*, from 258 — a fact not easily explained, since in 200 a Roman called Gaius had written of monuments to SS Peter and Paul at the sites of the later basilicas. An odd aspect of this cult is that the church of Rome was certainly not founded by any apostle, let alone Peter or Paul.

Another odd fact is that what looks like the earliest portrait of Peter (the only pre-Constantinian one as far as I know) is painted, faint but clear and strikingly skilful, on the wall of the *hypogeum* of the Aurelii, a heterodox site of which critics are very uncertain what to make, except that it is dateable before 275. After Constantine the fourth century offers scores of Petrine portraits and New Testament scenes involving him — on catacomb walls and sarcophagi: one of the latter called 'Three Monograms' and showing the Denial (with a cock that looks more like a duck) was found in the excavations under the *confessio*.

Damasus, a vigorous protagonist of the claims of the see of Rome, was equally energetic in promoting the cult of martyrs and especially of Peter and Paul, putting up sonorous inscriptions everywhere, and arguing that this and not its pagan past was the city's real claim to excellence.

This triumphalism bore an obvious relation (or counter-relation) to that of the Emperors, and not surprisingly a leading theme in Peter-and-Paul iconography was the *traditio legis* — Christ, youthful or bearded, handing the scroll of laws to Peter, who sometimes carries the cross to show that his title to his charge is his martyrdom. (A sarcophagus at the Basilica on the Via Appia shows Christ *blessing* Peter as he is led away to execution. A Vatican fourth-century coin shows Peter and Paul with beards stylised like an Assyrian relief, with the ☧ above them.)

The badge of the cross, familiar early in a disguised form — the anchor, the axe and the yardarm — became the great trophy of victory after Constantine, adopted in sermons and liturgy. The sixth-century hymns of Venantius Fortunatus are still familiar at Passiontide. A Lateran sarcophagus of 350 shows the ☧ flanked by scenes of the Passion, and the cross, combined with other symbols, appears in mosaics, diptychs and at last separately carved or wrought; it survives the iconoclastic crisis (e.g. at St Irene in Constantinople). The crucifixion-scene, with its shameful associations, is slower to establish itself. One of the first, if not the first, example is the curious panel on the door of St Sabina, about the same date as St Mary Major, where Christ and the two thieves appear nailed to a kind of gabled scaffolding. Perhaps earlier is the more conventional representation on an Italian ivory casket in the British Museum.

The 28 original cypress panels on the St Sabina door are a unique survival in situ. The temple in which Zechariah is struck dumb has Syrian-looking twin towers flanking a jewelled cross. In another panel Our Lady between SS Peter and Paul appears in the lower register, Christ in a circular garland, delivering the law, with the symbols of the evangelist in the upper.

The oriental influences in this door remind us that, long before it was made, *imperium* had been divided between East and West, the Bosphorus and Italy — not Rome but the north, Milan and then Ravenna, where the Western rulers established themselves from 402. It is here that we can most conveniently observe the transition from the Christian Roman to the Byzantine. What is called 'the mausoleum of Galla Placidia' (more likely a memoria of St Lawrence, who is there with his gridiron in mosaic) is one of the chief experiences of European travel. The well-shaped but plain brick exterior gives no hint of the glory within. The Good Shepherd mosaic, last example of a venerable Christian subject, gathers up the best of late antique elegance, but its rich, subtle glow points forward to the different splendours of Justinian's age, which are manifest hard by in S Vitale. Galla Placidia, half-sister of Emperor Honorius, was carried off by the Visigoth warrior Ataulf, but survived to return and commission this masterpiece, as well as the much-restored basilica of St John which looks no less clearly to Byzantium.

Yet it might be argued that the most moving monuments of Ravenna belong to the reign of the Ostrogothic King Theodoric, (493-529) who has come to be thought of as the type of the barbarian chief overwhelmed by a superior culture, wearing the purple and patronising the arts. Of his buildings in Ravenna the best known is the basilica he built next to his palace, which later came to be known as S Apollinare Nuovo. Theodoric was an Arian, but the mosaics surviving from his reign reinforce the view that there was no Arian iconography. On the other hand, the Madonna and Child attended by angels (towards whom the magi and the grave Virgins of Justinian's time process) shows clearly how well the dogma of Ephesus was accepted in Arian Ravenna. When Justinian drove out the Goths and this church's decoration was altered and extended, some figures were erased from in front of the mosaic of Theodoric's palace, but there is no reason to suppose that this was for theological reasons. Theodoric's basilica could be taken to illustrate the words of the poem:

> *. . . per te*
> *Barbari discunt resonare Christum*
> *Corde Romano.*
> (Through you
> the barbarians learn to praise Christ
> with a Roman heart.)

The two famous processions of virgins and martyrs which move down either wall of the nave belong to another age: they mark the triumphant return of Byzantium to Ravenna at a moment when the art of Justinian's age had matured. With the *martyrion* of S Vitale, they have behind them the splendours which the emperor added to Constantinople.*

There is no space here to deal fully with these, or to do more than mention the variety of influences — Hellenistic, Syrian, Persian, Roman — the subtlety, the passion for mathematics, geometry, optical theory, harmony of colour, line and shape, the careful calculation of effect that went into this high peak of artistic history. Some of the glory of Hagia Sophia has departed, and these 'monuments of unageing intellect', as Yeats brilliantly called them, can be as well studied in Ravenna as anywhere, and especially at S Vitale. Sophistication of architectural plan and design has rarely reached so far**, and no description is a substitute for moving about in it among the play of space and solid, light and shadow, a play echoed in the carving of the capitals. Only after this should one submit to the dazzling brilliance of the revetments, mosaic and marble.

This is the supreme word in the theology of empire. Old Testament type scenes, Abel, Abraham, Melchisedek, point to the Eucharist, but far from unobtrusively Justinian and Theodora with courtiers and the bishop come forward, empurpled and jewelled, with the offerings of bread and wine. It is hard to think that we are scarcely more than a century from the catacombs, and that already Benedict has founded Monte

---

* S Vitale may have been begun just before Theodoric's death but as an achieved work it belongs to the Age of Justinian.

** though a forerunner can be seen at S Lorenzo, Milan as early as the third quarter of the fifth century.

Cassino. We shall have a great deal more court religious art before the French revolution, but hardly any with such rich and varied resources of materials, skill and learned bureaucracy at its back. We need not exaggerate the width or depth of the religious feeling, as we tend to because the religious has survived better than the secular; in such a society there had to be scepticism and hedonistic conformism. But behind the magnificence was an idea, in part theological. Gervase Mathew has expressed it well:

> The Emperor's power was in no sense arbitrary. He was conceived as the sacred vice regent of God on earth. His sovereignty reflected God's omnipotence. But the divine omnipotence was conceived as an act of mind and love; all things were brought into being and kept in being by His knowledge of them. Therefore the Imperial sovereignty was an act of mind and love, exercised according to the unchanging law of reason and finding its fulfilment in the essential Imperial virtue of philanthropia, the love of man. Imperial largesse was an expression of this philanthropia. Each gift was an act of love and mind. And so, in a fashion hard for Westerners to understand, each gift was also an Imperial 'theophany' by which the mind and love of the Emperor visibly became manifest, even along the farthest boundaries of his Empire.[2]

It was dramatised liturgy, it was imperial propaganda, and the one flowed, shimmering and catching every glint of light, into the other. As a setting for equally splendid costume and ritual, under blue, starry domes and half domes, it dazzled and overawed, like the baroque later, and captured the Russians for the Orthodox faith. Men from simple, stern places thought it was heaven come on earth. 'The kingdom of God is come upon you,' but not the *basileia* of the New Testament; the saving event, the leaven, the mustard seed is now an enveloping, sometimes suffocating theocracy.

But we look at a stone grill, made of vines, among which

---

(2) Gervase Mathew, *Byzantine Aesthetics* (John Murray 1963), p. 64..

the peacocks of immortality perch, contemplating a cross, the whole growing out of a chalice, and we see that the quiet symbolism of the catacombs has been taken up into this intricate display, which could make dizzy those who approached it with the aesthetics of the waxwork show, give maturer delight to the alert eye and the geometrical mind, but offered most to those gifted to discern the divine. 'Invisibilia enim ejus per ea quae facta sunt intellecta conspiciuntur'. ('For the invisible things of God are seen and understood through his works.')

Perhaps contemplation was easier with smaller works, the ivories, the purple *codices* of the gospels, the medals or silver dishes and eventually the wax-painted icons found from the end of the fifth century. Apse-mosaics, a pantocrator in a cupola, would not easily excite devotion; a portable image could, and at last this might get out of hand. That it did so is the reasonable explanation of that crisis in the relations of theology and art, the iconoclast troubles. The idea than an image multiplied a presence and called for a relative veneration, which might decline into ambiguity, derived perhaps as much from the tradition of imperial portraits as from Christian iconography and sentiment. Julian the Apostate argued that 'He who loves the emperor delights to see the emperor's statue', and went on to extend the argument to the fear and trembling aroused by the images of the gods from the unseen world. The cultivated thought that to fail altogether to see the artistic image as a vehicle to the invisible was to be aesthetically obtuse — but this is far from entailing worship or veneration.

But when popular legends grew of the miraculous origins of some images (the madonnas attributed to St Luke would make him as prolific as his later namesake Luca Fa Presto), they attracted some of the devotion lavished on martyrs' relics. In crowded cities especially, this could become extravagant. The reaction was extravagant too, when the Emperor Leo III issued an edict for the destruction of all images of Christ, his Mother, saints and angels. Yet it cannot be seen as a root-and-branch attack on art applied to religion. More plausibly it was a return to an earlier tradition of symbols, which some at least saw as more reverent. It was not a deep doctrinal dispute — both sides appealed to Chalcedon and to the past. But the challenge of the Incarnation to art having once been met triumphantly by genius, there could be no going back. The second council of Nicaea (787) with studied moderation carefully discriminated between degrees of honour and worship, vindicated images as aids to devotion and, without eliminating the possibilities of abuse or of renewed revulsion in the future, assured the prosperity of religious art for rather less than another millennium.

The defeat of iconoclasm gave greater prestige than ever to the graphic arts. Sight became queen of the senses — not to be deposed for more than two centuries. Aesthetic theories ramified. Islamic influence enriched art further though only obliquely in the religious sphere. Against this the very prestige of the graphic arts brought rigidity to iconographic rules and other conventions which finally became oppressive, thought it has been part of our defective sympathy with the eastern Orthodox tradition to exaggerate the Egyptian static character of its art, and to contrast it too sharply with those western medieval developments which it sometimes anticipated (cf. chap. 6, p.68). We cannot here follow the long, later history of Byzantine art but its continuing influence in the West, through Byzantine 'outposts' or in places where it was taken into new medieval cultures as in Sicily, will assume special interest as theologically and otherwise East and West tragically drift further apart.

4
THE BARBARIAN FUSION

Byzantine architecture and art reflected a unified society in which secular and sacred were a good deal more distinct than we suppose from its art, because so little secular art has survived: Church and Empire, though aspects of one society, were by no means indistinguishable or without tension between them.

Yet the art was the art of a unified society and the unification, or the domination of art by religion, became more marked in later medieval phases of Byzantine society. Even when shrunken and again beleaguered by the conquests of Islam, it was a society where immense resources of official patronage allowed the development of a highly sophisticated, intellectualized art and architecture, drawing on many styles and traditions, reflecting the theological achievement of the Church of the Eastern Fathers which was at the same time an 'imperial' theology, though not a Caesaro-papist one.

The general impulse behind monasticism was a mistrust of all this, though much less necessarily a mistrust of the intellectual element. Eastern monasticism took several forms, some of which manifested more readily than others the dangers of an asceticism which at once contracted out of society and became almost a popular craze.

In the West (where the best insights of eastern monasticism had solid effect through, for example, John Cassian and spread as far as Ireland) it was no accident that some of the earliest experiments were associated with Augustine, whose 'two cities' were certainly not identifiable with any earthly institutions but were the result of choices made by men — *Pondus meum amor meus, eo feror quocumque feror.* ('My weight is my love; in all my movements I am moved by it.') Still less of an accident was it that Gregory the Great, who wrote the life of Benedict and was his great prop, would learn no Greek and heartily disliked New Rome with all its works and pomps.

The old cliches retain their truth, that monasticism was the carrier of the culture of the ancient world to the new Christian society, but it is questionable whether, where the arts are concerned, Benedictine monasticism, or any other, would have done this of its own inner resources. With the exception of Rome, which had several Greek-speaking or Syrian popes in the second half of the seventh and the first half of the eighth centuries (S Maria Antiqua belongs to the second of these periods), what was decisive after the Byzantine impulse was greatly diminished elsewhere in the West with the death of Justinian and the reversal of his conquests by the Lombards, was the impact of the gospel on the barbarians and the resumption, in so different a form of the imperial theme in the Carolingian renaissance.

The migratory peoples who overran the Empire had already considerable skill in decorating small portable objects, especially for war, and they were very fond of gold. But with them representation as distinct from decoration rarely went beyond the animal kingdom. Their first attempts after their conversion dealt with subjects like Daniel and the lions — the sort of biblical thriller that would have a quick appeal and could be chased on, say, a buckle. (There is a sixth-century one at Lausanne.) But even more serious attempts to emulate the Christian-classical models generally reverted to the abstract, which was handled with greater assurance, as a comparison of a purely ornamental page of the Lindisfarne gospel (A D 700) with one of its evangelist-portraits shows. There is more affinity with the Coptic and Syrian than with the Italian or Byzantine, and indeed there were likely contacts through the monasteries. These 'illuminated' gospel-manuscripts, in beautiful script, travelled freely, though only churchmen could read them.

The new peoples were obviously less likely to put up and decorate buildings, and the bulk of what they did put up was in wood and has disappeared. But pre-Carolingian church-building has been undervalued, especially considering the horrors of the time. The Lombards in the seventh century even had guilds of master builders around Como (the bent was to last there till the late baroque age) while seventh century Visigothic churches in Spain, Byzantine inspired, are moving things to discover in remote places, built as they were not long before the Moorish flood passed over them. In the hey-day of the Anglo-Saxon Church, which contributed so much to the Carolingian renaissance, there is evidence that there was building (at Hexham, for example) much more ambitious than the rather gloomy survivals in the North-East. The learning of Bede had its artistic counterpart.

What is clear in these and other places is that in difficult times the tradition of honouring God and serving religion by human skills was quickly assimilated and tenaciously held. If there was any 'theology of crisis' it did not manifest itself negatively in the arts. Probably already the feeling was that in a precarious world everything should be done to make the church building and ritual manifest as far as possible the eternity of the spiritual.

Charlemagne's campaign to revive learning and the arts was called *renovatio* — it was an attempt to recapture the imperial legacy even in its pre-Constantinian form, but also to put it at the service of the spread of the scriptures, in the spirit of Augustine's *De Doctrina Christiana*. Charlemagne's chief adviser was Alcuin from Britain, where that aim had remained more persistent and self-conscious, though not without its bitter enemies such as Aldhelm of Malmesbury. Charlemagne's position rested on the achievements of Charles Martel in halting Islam, on the piety of Pepin, on his own military campaigns and on the gradual swing of policy of the papacy which culminated in the famous 'coronation'. This last embarassed and worried Charlemagne, but not because he had any inhibitions about becoming an emperor.

His palace chapel at Aachen was a simplified version of Justinian's S Vitale, but it also had borrowings from classical Rome. In concentrating on this as a 'pathetic' imitation of the imperial past, historians have again made the mistake of judging too much by what survives. What we know of churches that were built or planned at Centula, at Corvey, at Paderborn, and at St Gall but which have disappeared or were never carried out, shows much more the originality of the northern 'renaissance'. It is clearer still from such works as the Utrecht Psalter, or the 'Crystal of Lothar' in the British Museum, which illustrates in energetic strip cartoon the story of Susannah. Here the Mediterranean legacy is receiving not the flattery of imitation (whatever the proclaimed intentions may have been) but a powerful shot in the arm. We are watching the results, as pregnant for art as for theology, of the barbarian's fresh and eager perception of the Christian message, revitalising a 'cultural inheritance' which was tired and could soon have expired. If Charlemagne's brief achievement, in Lord Clark's phrase, assured that Roman civilisation came through by the skin of its teeth, it did so not by embalming it but by giving it a blood transfusion. Classical motives were used more freely in Christian work than they had been even in the fourth century — you find them even in a Munich ivory of the Passion — but Lord Clark has well pointed out how the Cross of Lothar at Aachen illustrates the new Christian empire: the one side encrusted with filigree, jewels and a cameo of Augustus; the other flat silver with a simple but marvellous engraving of the crucifixion.

What is already evident by the end of the Carolingian era is the beginning of a distinctively Christian art in the West — something which is born of and draws its life from the gospel and the Church — from a Christian sensibility. It will take some time to come to flower. Many things are lacking which are necessary to a great artistic revival. Even after the last flicker of the Carolingian period there is a long period of incubation. But when that is over art, though well aware of its debt to the past, always ready to refresh itself deeply at the classical springs, is no longer looking backward but forward. It is a prime instrument and expression of the creation of a new religious society.

The incubation period was long for many reasons. After the breakdown of the Carolingian enterprise, Western Europe was besieged — from the north (Scandinavia), from the east (Magyars and Arabs), in the Mediterranean (Islam). It was poverty stricken, thinly-populated, almost without trade, its

46

links with the true world of learning, the East, tenuous. It has been said with some truth that, from the time Theodoric slew Boethius to the time Anselm travelled north from Italy to Normandy — five centuries — there was only one theologian of consequence in the West, Eriguena, and he was the one who knew Greek.

For a long time western theological concern lay largely in the area of what we should now call 'Church and Society'. The notion of a Western Empire existing by the blessing of the papacy alienated the Greeks without convincing the western claimants themselves, and without giving more than occasional fleeting promise of the kind of unified western leadership necessary to provide general security. The achievements of the German kings, though important enough to bolster their claims to *imperium*, were not enough to offset the growing division between German-speaking and Romance-speaking Europe and between North and South. Some of the most powerful forces for recovery in the West during the tenth and the first half of the eleventh centuries — Venetian leadership in the recovery of Eastern trade, the genius of the newly-converted Normans for purposeful pilgrimage, conquest, assimilation and organization, above all the monastic energy most famously exemplified in Cluny — worked in calm dissociation from the imperial idea.

The papacy's prestige was less dependent on achievement. Before the reforms which in the second half of the eleventh century brought the papacy effective centralised authority, Rome was the chief of a constellation of shrines in a Europe where relics were still more important than regulations for protecting men and property. Rome, as the shrine of Peter and Paul, was a centre of pilgrimage; against this its squalor, decay and feudal stagnation counted little — to the tenth-century poet it was *Roma nobilis, orbis et domina* ('noble Rome, the mistress of the world').

But if Rome's prestige rested on the relics belonging to an authentic past, other cities and monasteries, as Europe recovered, lost no time in acquiring relics to ensure their future. In 827 two Venetian merchants smuggled the body of St Mark out past the Moslem customs at Alexandria under a load of pork and carried it back to the lagoon to begin the history of the great church there. As with so many other such shrines, a fire (in 976) gave the chance for it to be rebuilt, the body having been miraculously revealed after the fire. At the height of the quarrel between Henry IV and Gregory the Byzantine five-domed church, modelled on the legendary Holy Apostles of Constantinople, was put up.

At the pioneering reform monastery of Fleury on the Loire, there rested the body of St Benedict himself, collected from the ruins of Monte Cassino (destroyed by maurauders in the later seventh century). Taking occasional shelter from the Vikings within the walls of Orleans, the relics became the nucleus of a great monastery and school, and in the second half of the eleventh century one of the finest Romanesque churches (second only to Cluny) was built over them. It still stands and has been used again by monks since 1944.

The takeover of southern Italy from the Byzantines by the Normans was signalised by sailors from Bari stealing the relics of St Nicholas from Myra in Anatolia and bringing them home; a noble Romanesque church and precinct (giving rise to a whole school of architecture and sculpture) was reared over the spot where they landed.

Such examples could be multiplied endlessly. They point to the leading characteristic of Romanesque art. The 'white mantle of churches', which Raoul Glaber said covered Europe after the year 1000, were mainly focal points of local loyalties; the chief force behind them was the monastic revival, but a monasticism caught up widely and intimately in the country-side, which learnt from the monks its religion and much else besides. The monasteries which built the high Romanesque churches were not refuges from the world; rich warlike donors did not want this — they wanted in the neighbourhood power-ful, durable expressions of a corporate religion which were also of social and economic weight.

Though the monastic reform and multiplication, especially from Cluny, lent weight to the gigantic late eleventh-century effort of Church reform, and provided much of the literary ammunition in the triumph of *sacerdotium* over *imperium*, the arts reflect little or nothing of this revolution, except in manuscript illuminations. Though the ninth-century Carolingian Bibles were still picturing crowned emperors, and the German art of the Ottonian period still retained an imperial *gravitas* and monumentality, imperial religion as Byzantium still understood it was a lost cause in the West, though it was to be a long time a-dying. On the whole the arts reflect this truth, because they reflect little of the intense struggle from which medieval papal power emerged, though it was a fundamental crisis in the theology of politics. What is more impressive is that they reflect equally little of the expansion and consolidation of papal power. From Hildebrand to Innocent III only half a dozen churches (and only two of them important) were built in Rome and though some of the older ones were rebuilt or embellished, Rome has never had Romanesque monuments to compare with those of, say, Cologne before the war, or Burgundy. We know little of what Gregory VII looked like except from literary sources; Innocent III has been immortalised by Giotto only because he sponsored St Francis; and the pope whose statue sits in the solemn imperial manner outside his palace at Anagni is the one who pushed the claims of the medieval papacy to extremes and saw the real end of it all — Boniface VIII.

An exception is the cycle of frescoes in the chapel of St Sylvester near the Roman church of Quattro Coronati. Decidedly Byzantine in manner and dating from the last phase of the struggle with the Hohenstaufen, they depict episodes from the legend of Constantine selected to bolster the Donation. Mention might be made here of the *Ottonianium*, the splendid purple parchment lettered in gold (very Byzantine) by which Otto the Great at his coronation in 962 recognised the papal sovereignty over the patrimony of St Peter.

What were the themes of Romanesque art? Apart from the general architectural ambition, that the Church should embody eternity in a world which even in the twelfth century was for the majority still poor and precarious, it is hard to be general among such a rich regional variety. Many themes — the portrayal of the seasons, the signs of the zodiac — had no direct theological reference. Others — series of saints, prophets, biblical episodes — were not new. Others again were grotesque — the weird hybrids devouring each other, the monsters of Cluniac art that St Bernard railed against in a much-quoted sermon. They all reflected the monastic mind, encyclopedic rather than systematic. Theorists of allegory will laboriously explain every one. Two general explanations may be considered.

In a violent, fear-ridden age like the tenth century, the Apocalypse was a favourite book, and the Last Judgment became and remained a favourite theme, especially for the lunettes above church doors. Perhaps illiterate and ill-disciplined people, plenty of whom could be found within the larger family (farmworkers and military retainers) of a great monastery, needed to have their consciences bludgeoned. Perhaps the artist did something to exorcise his own and the communal mind with his chisel or his brush. But leaving aside the monstrosities, which in some places (Normandy and England, for example) were subdued and formalised and in others hardly appeared at all, the Christ who at first dominates romanesque art is a stern judge, before whom devils and damned alike quail, and whom even the saved look at with awe rather than love. This also reflects the theology of redemption before it was revolutionised by Anselm's *Cur Deus Homo* — a feudal theology, in which man watched powerless while God conquered, or we might rather say outwitted, the devil. Anselm, explaining our redemption in the vicarious suffering of the God-man, the first-born of the new creation, opened the way theologically for a new Christian art, a way to be much broadened by St Bernard and St Francis.

But if at Anselm's death this lay still some time ahead, artistic intuition here and there had already anticipated him. We have mentioned Lothar's cross (p.46). Even in the tenth century art tells us what histories do not, that men were beginning to deepen their feeling for the mysteries of the faith, to enter into the passion of Christ with human sympathy. But it took time for this to dominate. An eleventh-century Bur-

50

gundian crucifix in the Louvre shows our Lord on the cross still crowned with a gold crown, a hieratic figure from the past, but through the stylised technique of the gilded bronze an intense feeling forces its way.

To follow out this change of theology and sensibility belongs to the next chapter. Returning to the eschatological theme, we must ask whether the crowded chaos of so many damnation-scenes was really expected simply to make the blood curdle. It is said that the Last Judgment over the main door of Autun cathedral (carved 1130-1135) was saved from the revolutionaries in 1793 because the classical-minded canons had years before walled up the distasteful object. I find it hard to believe that the sculptor (Gislebert) who had carved the nude Eve lolling so sophisticatedly behind her fig-branch could have expected us to take his busy, grinning demons, fiddling the scales in which the souls are weighed, as solemnly as the canons did. The doubts multiply when we turn to another twelfth-century treatment of the same theme in a very different world — the island of Torcello near Venice, where the cathedral was decorated by mosaic workers, perhaps from Venice. Opposite the marvellous apse with its majestic *theotokos* is a mosaic in which two elegant Byzantine angels with long rods poke away at the flames where bejewelled emperors, princesses, a bishop, monks, a moorish chief are half-buried. Little blue-winged devils are playing a sort of ball game with the heads of the damned. There are even more disconcerting elements in this theological fantasy, which is clearly a case of an eastern artist assimilating a western tradition, but not very reverently.

Perhaps we should remember that this was the time at which men were beginning to feel the full weight of the medieval Church. They were baptized into it before they were aware of anything, and it was as pervasive as the air they breathed until the day of their death. The eleventh-century Church had with a powerful effort checked simony, clerical marriage, lay control. It had largely thrown off the grip of the clan, that dark, primitive, litigious instinct men have to cling to, perpetuate, increase the power and property of their blood.

51

But the effort was generated and achieved through a single-minded, grimly logical, clericalist view of the Church which had its own dangers and was to produce a violent revulsion nearly half a millennium later. At the time when some of the noblest Romanesque churches were being built and adorned, St Bernard, who railed against the art of Cluny, railed also against the papal court. Perhaps he could hardly suspect that the artists whose fantasies covered capitals and lintels were really speaking with him in another language. Artists caught up in a great machine find their own safety-valves.

The point must not be exaggerated. The Autun Last Judgment is dominated by the awesome Christ dwarfing all other figures; but it also dwarfs the sense of terror conveyed by the devils and the damned. I am not convinced that Gislebert's heart is in the business of frightening the wits out of the simple-minded.

The sculpture in the corresponding place at Vezelay (rather earlier) is similarly dominated by a huge central Christ-figure, but here he is serenely dispensing the Spirit, as rays of light from his hands, to his apostles, who are sent to the world to preach the gospel. Here the artist's fantasy has all gone into picturing the strange peoples who will be offered the light of the Gospel.

That moralistic sculpture was not always naive at this time is clear from a figure (to take one example) of an adultress on the 'goldsmiths' door' at Santiago di Compostella. This blowsy, half-naked drab, weak and stupid, carrying the skull of her lover in her lap, would frighten any adult more than a wallful of grinning demons: it would make an apt illustration for Webster or Ford or better perhaps Ben Jonson.

Perhaps the overpowering conventional life of the successful monasteries was weighing on men: on those who embraced it without positive vocation, like the unwilling nun in the famous twelfth-century poem, and on those who worked whether as soldiers, peasants, artists or craftsmen within a powerful organisation which they felt now to be constricting rather than liberating.

It is notable that two of the great poems of the time, which look forward to the next life, Bernard of Morlaix's 'Hora novissima, tempora pessima' and Abelard's 'O quanta qualia' look forward to rest, tranquillity, serene pastures, sabbath succeeding sabbath. If eschatological verse gives the hint, secular verse is much more outspokenly critical or even derisive of the already ponderous establishment. Theologically we hear of the subversive, heretical forms this rejection took, as with Peter of Bruys (d 1126) or Henry of Lausanne (d 1145), the anarchical puritan preachers who rejected art, crucifixes, churches, sacraments, and were condemned as heretics or shunned as subverters. But there was plenty of criticism and satire that stemmed from a complete acceptance of the Church as a supernatural or at least unshakeable reality. Medieval living conditions had long made poets eloquent in sighing for a return of spring. The longing could easily transfer itself to the world of the spirit. By the middle of the twelfth century there were signs of spring to be welcomed, and they were not deceptive.

THE CHRISTIAN SOCIETY

The title is not a value judgment but covers a period, not much more than a century, during which Christian belief and organization dominated European society as it never has before or since — though not without fierce opposition, especially as far as organisation was concerned. An essay like this, however short, must attend to the period in some detail for several reasons.

1) The Church's concern to provide a programme (as well as patronage and other forms of encouragement) for artists reached its peak during this period.

2) The linking of theology and the arts was more thorough at this period than at any other (again, not a value judgment).

3) The results were at their best immensely impressive and form a notable part of our civilised heritage, though from some points of view we are more critical of them than our immediate ancestors were.

4) The theology of the period (or what it was believed to be) until recently dominated modern Catholic thinking. So did the art, though more superficially (or perhaps one should say more obviously superficially: we still had genuine 'Gothic' masterpieces handy to compare with Gothic revival and mostly one had to be a simpleton or an eccentric to be taken in. It was trickier with theology.)

The chapter covers two historic 'styles', the mature Romanesque and the Gothic. (This word is not satisfactory but this is no place to fuss about it.) It is useful to point to some general features of the period straight away.

1) The emphasis shifts from the monastery to the cathedral and the township, where the universities grow up. Romanesque was *mainly* the style of one, Gothic of the other. Though monasteries long outlasted Romanesque and in other ways the lines are blurred, the only monastic order that put a distinctive stamp on Gothic art, the Cistercians, did so in a way that remained outside the main stream.

2) In religious life there was a shift away from the dominance of Cluny — the Romanesque order *par excellence* — or rather several shifts represented by the Cistercians and the Augustinians and later by the friars, who were just as much a reaction against the Cistercians, if not more.

3) There was a gradual shift from the aristocratic to the popular, evident in art, though it is easy to exaggerate or distort it, as will be seen.

4) Connected with this, the imperial theme almost disappears, and where it survives appears as conservative and old-fashioned. The majesty of Christ becomes of quite another order, and his humanity arouses quite new interests. (There is a Byzantine ivory in Paris showing *Christ* crowning the Emperor Romanus (920-44) and his consort. This was already long unthinkable in the West.) The struggle of Papacy and Empire had little impact on the arts, though some history-manuals would make you think it overshadowed the middle age. This at least suggests that the papal power advanced at this period more by the power of the papal courts than by its impact on general imagination.

5) The advance of the *studium generale* (of the universities) and the theological dominance of Paris gradually narrowed and concentrated learned energies. To put it bleakly, there was more future in theology and canon law than in more humane pursuits. It is not evident that theology entirely gained from this; it will be interesting to consider how far the arts escaped the process and how far they gained or lost by it.

6) Byzantine influence, though it did not disappear from the West, was faintest in those areas in which art was most energetic and innovating.

To retake our bearings we might look at the single example of a great church which is very representative — that of Vezelay. It was founded in the post-Carolingian confusion by a feudal hero, Girart de Rousillon, on the top of its hill after a monastery which he had established in the valley had been destroyed by the Northmen. At the beginning of the reform period (latter eleventh century) it was alleged to have received the relics of St Mary Magdalene from Provence. It also became an assembly point for the Santiago pilgrimage. Hence the church was enlarged (1096-1104) during the first Crusade. In 1120 on the feast day, 22 July, it was burnt down (a frequent disaster in the Romanesque period.) But rebuilding began at once, and when St Bernard preached the second Crusade there in 1146, in the presence of Louis VII, it was almost ready. Later the monks, attracted by the new Gothic style, pulled down the choir and rebuilt it, and this was finished in 1215 — the year of Magna Carta and the fourth Lateran Council. By the end of our period other relics of the Magdalene had been 'discovered' in Provence and Vezelay was already in decline.

Nothing is more characteristic or reflects better the fever of energy of this century and a half. From the time that the third but last church of Cluny (a marvel of which sadly only a fragment remains) was completed in 1130, a moment when Gothic was already evolving in the North, to the building of St Urbain at Troyes (1262), we have in France a flow of intellectual and artistic energy which spread everywhere and left a stamp on artistic and architectural thinking for centuries. It is a period of restless and vigorous experiment with elements hardly any of which were new and some very old, but which were now fused in a new fire of thought and feeling.

In examining the theological connections of this it is easier to take the great buildings separately from their decoration, though without compromising the unity of the two. It is easy to show a series of parallels, chronological and topographical, between the phases of intellectual and architectural development. The cathedrals where the architects and artists experimented were also the centres of schools, Paris, Chartres, Laon. Men capable of designing cathedrals (one of the later ones was called 'Doctor' on his tombstone) were certainly capable of talking with the intellectuals of the schools where *disputatio* was breathed in with the air.

Erwin Panofsky has shown (I think convincingly) that the same habits of mind governed both activities. He focuses on two characteristic aims, *manifestatio* and *concordantia*. The first might be translated as 'elucidation', the second as 'harmonisation'.

To follow this argument we must rid ourselves of romantic notions of Gothic cathedrals as containers for the vaguely mystical, for 'dim religious light'. St Thomas who saw beauty as splendour of *form* (in his sense) shining through the proportional parts of matter, did not live in Paris for nothing; 'the senses delight in things duly proportional,' he said, 'as something akin to themselves, for the sense, too, is a kind of reason, as is every cognitive power.' (ST 1, qu. v, art. 4, ad 1) If faith could be elucidated by reason, both could be elucidated by imagination stimulated by the senses.

This bringing of all the faculties within an ordered scheme of elucidation, in which the final impetus comes from faith, might be the programme of the Gothic designer. Though the contrast with the Romanesque programme, conceived as the accumulation of self-contained units, can I think, be pressed too far, it is true that a new grasp of totality and a desire to pull buildings together, to manifest a logical coherence and an organic interdependence and progression between the precisely articulated parts, is strongly marked in Gothic. The cross-section of the main pier finally 'expresses' (manifests) all the structural members that spring from it, the facade expresses what lies behind it. The athletic flying buttresses both enhance the space enclosed and point to illuminated space.

The result, at last, combines rationality and *elan*, a kind of harmonising of faith and reason expressed in architectural terms. The ancient battle between 'aesthetic' and 'functional' interpretation seems pointless. Successful functioning is subsumed in elegance and clarity of visual logic — *'id quod visum placet'*, which is Aquinas' other definition of beauty.

Yet perfection is not achieved without tussles, dialectic as the contemporary term was, the second habit of mind to which Panofsky draws attention. Today we might call it 'problem-solving'. Gratian's *Decretum*, Abelard's *Sic et Non*, the structure of St Thomas' *Quaestiones Disputatae*, all accept elucidation as wrenching harmony out of discordance; to follow the same process in a great building-campaign needs a careful comparison of many buildings. The individual building can very rarely reveal it — it must always be at best a provisional solution. But the play of dialectic as well as the upward aspiration of faith becomes fascinatingly evident when one watches the development of Early and High Gothic architecture. Walls, windows, vaults, piers, capitals, west front are pushed and pulled about in search of perfection, and though there are seeming backward as well as forward steps, the prevalent effect is a progressive disembodiment until what is left is a taut, tense frame suffused with light and colour. *Concordantia* is achieved, but the dialectic is still evident in the result. As Panofsky says:

> A man imbued with the Scholastic habit would look upon the mode of architectural presentation, just as he looked upon the mode of literary presentation, from the point of view of *manifestatio*. He would have taken it for granted that the primary purpose of the many elements that compose a cathedral was to ensure stability, just as he took it for granted that the primary purpose of the many elements that constitute a *Summa* was to ensure validity.
>
> But he would not have been satisfied had not the membrification of the edifice permitted him to re-experience the very processes of architectural composition just as the membrification of the *Summa* permitted him to re-experience the very processes of cogitation. To him, the panoply of shafts, ribs, buttresses, tracery, pinnacles, and crockets was a self-analysis and self-explication of architecture much as the customary apparatus of parts, distinctions, questions, and articles was, to him, a self-analysis and self-explication of reason.[1]

The creative outflow of Gothic is agreed to have begun with the choir of the abbey of St Denis, about 1147. Its abbot, Suger, was a monk much immersed in the world, a friend of the King, and for a time his regent, a practical man and an impresario rather than a theologian, but he had one clear theological idea, that art, as an imitation of creation, was a

---

(1) E. Panofsky, *Gothic Architecture and Scholasticism* (Thames & Hudson 1957), pp. 58-9.

sacramental activity, mustering nature's bounties to reveal and praise God's glory. For him the talent of everybody — architect, sculptor, goldsmith or mere collector — could contribute to this. The ideas of his contemporary, St Bernard — equally a man of affairs — were different.

We have seen what he thought of Cluniac fancies, and for the Cistercians the new style offered scope for austerity. Thus it was the Cistercian monasteries which first spread a genuine international 'Gothic', beautiful of line, bare of ornament, dry and golden like Burgundy's white wine, but most attractive to the *sensus quae est quaedam ratio*[2] (sense, which is a form of reason). Yet the style remained outside the main current and the original Cistercian impulse did not last long. Even in England (the true home of the rich later development of Gothic), where figure-sculpture never made much headway, the restrained Early English gave way to the curved lines and luxuriant foliation of the fourteenth century.

On its French home-ground, classical Gothic launched the most comprehensive decorative schemes architecture had yet seen. Here the influence, or the direction, of the theologian was more diffuse, and to plot it we should have to go far beyond the austere dialecticians who flicker in and out of modern manuals, none of which would take us far in reading a great Gothic portal or stained-glass window. It is the ambitious encyclopedia, the *imago mundi*, which is the artist's quarry rather than the more narrowly theological *Summa*. It is one of these compendia of universal knowledge, the *Speculum Majus* of Vincent of Beauvais, that Émile Mâle used as a frame for exploring the forest of Gothic decorative art.

It has four books: the Mirror of Nature, a kind of commentary on the seven biblical days of creation, with heavy emphasis on symbolism, especially of flora and fauna; the Mirror of Instruction, which covers both labour and polite learning ('work delivers man from want, and instruction from

---

(2) ". . . each and all of these hardy ascetics carried in his bosom a humanist who by no means wanted to die." E. Gilson, *The Mystical Theology of St Bernard* (1940), p. 63.

ignorance'); the Mirror of Morals which illustrates virtues and vices; and the Mirror of History which covers the Bible, the Apocrypha, the lives of the saints and what there was of secular history. Vincent's work did not appear until near the end of the classical Gothic period, but being a compilation of long accepted things it is an excellent key.

The first book — a crucial one from the interpretation point of view — needs to be supplemented by an earlier work, Honorius of Autun's *Speculum Ecclesiae*, through the medium of which the medieval 'bestiaries' exercised most of what influence they had on medieval art. It is a fantasy that every animal or plant carved or painted had a symbolic intent — much of the exuberant nature work was an exercise in what our present jargon would call 'celebration'. But Mâle shows in some detail that Honorius' work, really a re-hash of sermons which by ingenious symbolism makes the whole world witness to the truths of Faith, lay behind many of the programmes supplied to artists. These programmes prescribed the substance, but left a good deal also to the artists' fancy.

A good deal of Honorius' animal-symbolism was of course as old as Christian art itself. A collection like the *Physiologus*, perhaps as old as the second century, used by the Fathers, though eventually condemned by a pope, continued to be drawn on freely. But the ancient repertory was at times enlarged and supplementary meanings were given: for example, the four ancient symbols of the evangelists were a great temptation to ingenious elaborators. Some animal-figures came straight from scripture, like the asp and basilisk, lion and dragon on which Christ stood as at Amiens (cf. Ps 91.13).

Numbers, of course, had been a terrible weakness ever since the times of the Fathers. Nothing betrays our remoteness from the medieval mind (something often overlooked in seminaries) more than our difficulty in taking seriously the mysticism of numbers. Twelve, the number of the apostles, taken to represent the Church, consisted of three (the Trinity, hence Spirit) multiplied by four (the elements, hence Matter). But the number seven was the most obsessive: vices, virtues, the ages of man, liberal arts, petitions of the Our Father, planets, days of the week, musical tones, and so on — something could be made out of all of them. Baptismal fonts were often octagonal; so the number eight represented starting again — spiritual re-birth, new life. It was believed that the body united with the soul forty-six days after conception; so Honorius explained this by adding together the serial numbers of the Greek letters for 'Adam'. The pitch this had reached by the late middle ages is shown by the fact that Henry Suso, a very respectable mystic, used to cut his apple into four quarters, peel and eat three of them in the name of the Trinity, and eat the fourth unpeeled in honour of the infant Jesus, since little boys do not peel their apples.

By the time the sacraments came to be a theme of figurative art, the four rivers of paradise, which had been associated with the evangelists, were increased to seven.

These numbers were useful in decorating porches and windows, where symmetry was called for. For the months the round of the year's tasks provided images to go with the signs of the zodiac. Thus the life of the peasant was brought within the orbit of the liturgy. The liberal arts had been personified since the fifth century as girls appropriately dressed and equipped, in an allegory by Martianus Capella about the wedding of Mercury. (Dialectic was thin and shrewish with rolled hair denoting strings of syllogisms, carrying a serpent or scorpion to denote the wiles of sophistry and a hook for insidious argument.) Classical authors associated with the liberal arts sometimes get in.

Philosophy was shown, according to a vision that appeared to Boethius, as a woman with her head piercing the clouds. Also from Boethius came the wheel of Fortune in connection with the arts, implying ruefully that there was no money to be made out of them.

Moving on to the Mirror of Morals, the idea of a battle between vices and virtues, and hence that of personifying them, was very old, and had been given classical expression in the versified *Psychomachia* of Prudentius, where the combats are staged successively in an epic. This idea is used in simplified form with the virtue trampling on the opposite vice, but the Gothic artists largely abandon it in favour of more systematic treatment of symbolic or dramatic illustration. The virtues are merely symbolised, mostly by animals — a serpent for prudence, a lion for fortitude and so on. But the vices are dramatized with impressive economy. The opposite of Faith, idolatry, is a man worshipping a monkey; of Fortitude, a knight fleeing from a hare; of Perseverance, a runaway monk looking back at his monastery; of Obedience, a layman having a row with a bishop. It is interesting that while in the French schemes Charity never goes beyond almsgiving, in Italy, Giotto (Padua) and Orcagna (Or Sanmichele, Florence) portray simultaneously an act of mercy and the giving of the heart to God.

It is not as easy as the romantics thought to assess the impact of all this seeming didactic shorthand. We do not know a great deal about how medieval men looked at works of art and what we do know suggests that, as with the majority today, simple realism was the main criterion. But art always communicates at more than one level. Moreover distance and shadow obscured much. It may be that a comprehensive and harmonious scheme was a more conscious aim than a 'sermon in stone'.

There is poverty in a merely pragmatic view of religious art, which sees symbolic images as no more than an expedient to impress on untutored minds truths that developed intelligence grasps as clear and distinct ideas. A symbol, something sensible which points beyond itself to the unseen, the intangible, the spiritual, does not do so (within the field of faith) arbitrarily, as part of a casual code. It is richly associative, evocative; it links apprehension and reflection with feeling. Hence it is at least as important to the theologian as to the 'simple faithful', if the former is not to be as dry as dust. In a utilitarian or defensive age this need may be so starved that we cease to be aware of it. One of the great benefits of renewing strong links between theology and the Bible is that we are taken out of a world of flat rationalism into one where thought, image and feeling function properly in harmony.

From this point of view, medieval art (whose biblical side

we shall look at in a moment) is not a poor substitute for theology but an organic extension of it, taking account of man not as a dialectical machine but as a full person. There is of course an opposite danger which becomes sadly evident in the later middle ages, particularly in those areas where the Gothic spirit most ruled. Symbolism may luxuriate to the point where it defeats its end by wearying and confusing. It becomes the product of ingenuity which is laboured and at last perverse — part of a general neurotic excess which afflicts religion, and which neither bishops nor theologians can control. Image-making threatens to swamp theology and all orderly thinking. There is also too much money poured into pageantry, shows, luxurious feasts, para-liturgical activities; and the lords, ladies and bishops feasting or riding out to hunt in idyllic landscapes, the endless minutely observed birds, flowers, tiny pet dogs, and so on that fill Books of Hours, tapestries and pictures, begin by being gay and end by boring.

To go back to Vincent of Beauvais; his Mirror of History is dominated by the Bible, as is the decoration of the great cathedrals. There are examples of straightforward narrative sequences but usually the Old Testament is seen from the medieval theologian's point of view — concerned with those passages and persons which according to the various types of interpretations — historical, allegorical, tropological, anagogical — offer parallels with the New Testament and point forward to Christ. The prophets are pictured carrying grain to the mill which St Paul turns — they are not interesting in themselves nor are their books, but only as they speak of Christ, as the processions of 'prophets' did in the churches at Christmas. The drama and poetry of the Old Testament receives no great plastic expression, but the great figure-sculptors of Chartres and Amiens express the nobility of the prophets' vocation in their tall solemn statues.

The treatment of the gospels is similarly Christocentric, but the selection is strictly limited by the concerns of the theologian and of the major liturgical feasts. The iconography of the Nativity, for example, is dictated at first by the standard anthology of Bible commentary, the *Glossa Ordinaria*: Mary lies in contemplation, while the divine Infant is laid upon an altar. The more human type familiar to us comes later. There is an even stronger contrast between the high Gothic Crucifixions and the later versions with their strong emotional appeal. In a window at Bourges, to take a typical example, the crucifix is flanked by two female figures, the one crowned and holding up a chalice to catch the blood and water from Christ's side, the other blindfold, with a broken staff and a crown tumbling from her bowed head. They are the Church and the Synagogue. The iconography of the latter refers to a passage in Jeremiah. Altogether an ambiguous attitude to the Old Testament is revealed: it is the foundation of the New Testament, but also it is the book of the blinded Synagogue, obstinate and destined to collapse.

The theologians even take liberties with the gospel account — Mary is included in portrayals of the Ascension. The parables are surprisingly sparely used. The Good Samaritan offers an obvious chance for favourable comparison of the new with the old dispensation, and the wise and foolish virgins are linked with the Judgment. Dives and Lazarus and the Prodigal Son are the other choices.

By comparison the Apocrypha and the legends of the saints are freely quarried. Without claiming any critical standard for such works as the *Golden Legend*, we should remember that the word legend did not then have its current meaning: it simply meant 'improving reading'.

But nothing expresses so well as a great portal like Amiens or Chartres that all knowledge, from animal lore to the Bible, points to Christ. The revival of sculpture which had begun with the hesitant copying of illuminated manuscripts, ivories, oriental tapestries, and even coins, reached the heights in such figures as the Beau Dieu of Amiens. If it is possible for art to meet the challenge of the Incarnation, to express the divine in classical plastic terms, then this is as far as the challenge can be taken. The appeal to the senses is authentic but refined of all grossness: strength and beauty are without the disfigurement either of pride or of sentimentality. By comparison the greatest of the Greek idols are of the earth earthy.

Yet the equilibrium is a perilous one. Perhaps the remote Christs in the dome of Daphni and the apse of Cefalu were safer, though they too in the end were to be cheapened.

Suger of St Denis, who as much as anyone launched the Gothic enterprise, is unique in having left an account of what he did and why he did it. This is in part an apologia aimed at his contemporary and critic, the domineering St Bernard. But its interest is that it appeals to the supposed patron of his abbey, Denis the Areopagite (as mediated through John Scotus), for something like a total theory of sumptuary art. Number, proportion, order, splendour, everything that we discern in nature and call beautiful is a *light*, a *claritas*, reflecting and pointing to the supreme Light, the *luce intellectual' pien d'amore* as Dante was to call it. Natural and man-made beauty are the lights that lead us upwards, transport us (he borrows Scotus' own phrase) *more anagogico*.

I thought of it when I heard Paul VI, thanking a choir that had sung Hadyn's *Paukenmesse* for him, say that such experiences help us to 'keep our hearts fixed *ubi vera sunt gaudia*'. He was echoing a long tradition. Some even say (though I myself doubt it) that Bernard of Clairvaux railed against the Cluniac sculptures only because they attracted him too much. Certainly he used a marvellous phrase to describe them: '*deformis formositas, formosa deformitas*' (misshapen shapliness, shapely misshapenness). In any case, if he did not like his churches turned into picture-shows he considerably influenced the programmes of those who did, through the tradition of spirituality he established. It was by this rather than by his diatribes (though other factors played their part in that age of chivalry and courtly love) that he helped to change the ways of art.

ITALY AND RENAISSANCE

The great French Gothic impulse spread to many other places — to England especially, where its original restless, searching spirit perhaps lasted longer than anywhere else. But it never gripped the Italians in the same way. This can easily be seen by looking at an Italian Gothic building: (apart from the one or two Cistercian ones) it is far less complex than a French one — probably a vast hall designed to receive the crowds who, in the cities, flocked to hear the friars preach. It lacks structural boldness and even so has to be held together by visible iron bars. The horizontal is as evident as the vertical or more. It is altogether more human in scale and down-to-earth. An all-out late Gothic building like Milan cathedral, built by a rich tyrant, looks less at home than a Gothic revival cathedral built by American millionaires in an East coast city. The Rome of the great medieval popes (who indeed were too busy destroying the empire to find money for building) has only one very unconvincing Gothic church.

In South Italy and Sicily, conquered by Normans who resumed fitfully close relations with Byzantium, a rich stylistic brew — Arab, Byzantine, Romanesque, Gothic — developed in which the Gothic elements seemed even more ill at ease. Much the same was true in Venice or Padua. The humanist, Filarete, after admitting that he at first liked the 'modern manner' (meaning Gothic) until he got to know the Renaissance, later lamented that the pure Italian tradition had been swamped not only by invaders destroying the historic treasure, but also by Germans and French bringing in new artistic ways and making big churches that looked like tabernacles or censers. (He would not have got on with Pugin.)

On the other hand, if we begin looking for early signs of the next great revolution in architecture, the Renaissance, we can reach the point of wondering (quite wrongly) how much meaning is left in the term. On a hill above Florence is the church of S Miniato, with elegant, clean lines and round arches emphasised by the many coloured marbles plentiful in Tuscany. We are astounded to find that it was first built nearly fifty years before William of Normandy conquered England. (The baptistery of Florence is much the same in general appearance.) This building was even believed later to be classical in origin and certainly influenced Tuscan renaissance design.

But if the deliverance of Italian architecture represented as the Renaissance was from northern, Gothic shackles, that of painting was from the *maniera greca*, or southern Byzantine shackles. So at least thought the humanists. Petrarch and Boccaccio praised Giotto as the renewer, or reviver, of painting, not because he reverted to classical models (there scarcely were any for painters), but because he reverted to imitating nature. With sound instinct but without much evidence they rated him the peer of the ancients. Later humanists had a better, fuller understanding of Giotto, as did the fifteenth-century painters who resumed his tradition.

The *maniera greca* from which Giotto delivered painting was old-fashioned provincial Italian stuff, and today we would not find it necessary to praise Giotto by blackening Byzantine art, which in fact was undergoing similar renaissances from which Giotto may even have profited. Certainly the Roman mosaicist Torriti, Cavallini as both mosaicist and wall-painter and the great Sienese painter Duccio, all of them Giotto's older contemporaries, could be thought of as reviving or developing Byzantine forms as much as breaking out of their shackles. Just before Giotto was born, the Council of Lyons (1274) saw a determined attempt, though mistaken in method, to reunite eastern and western christendom by top-level negotiation. It has been argued that Franciscan 'innovations' in spirituality, like the crib and the theme of the Stabat Mater, had long been anticipated in the East. Both art and theology might have gained much if what Byzantine emperor and Roman negotiators agreed (it had been long and carefully prepared) had been accepted by clergy and people.

But here we are more concerned with what Italian innovators achieved than with the mistaken motives assigned for their innovations. The thirteenth century was a full one in Italian history too. It saw the climax and tragic end of the struggle between papacy and Hohenstaufen. The papacy with a feverish and expensive effort destroyed the empire (by the 1270's) but provided no alternative embodiment of the ideal order of christendom except the extension of its own operations, which after the end of the century were never again to have the same kind of authority. A sense that the great Gregorian dream of the single harmonious christian society, the single sacrament of Christ's presence, the seamless garment, was shattered, showed itself in many strange forms of protest.

At the beginning of the century the Franciscans and the Dominicans had been founded. The former order especially has appealed to most men ever since. Even before Francis's death the simple ideal of absolute renunciation was seen as incapable of a future without compromise. The result was a great church to house the saint's body, an institution which settled in the growing towns and universities with vast effect, but also a good deal of frustration which issued in utopian movements, taking up the dreams of a Third Age from the Calabrian abbot Joachim, offering in fact an unquiet, disorderly substitute for the imperial or Gregorian dream. Whatever Boniface VIII might say about the ancient hostility of laymen, they did not want this kind of protest any more than bishops did. The disrepute, the heresy trials in which all this ended, meant that eschatological expectations and awareness of the Holy Spirit, as anything but a guarantor of impersonal officialdom, sank very low in the western Church — another thing which aggravated the tragedy of the failures of reconciliation with the Church of the now doomed Eastern empire.

It is tempting to link this with the very uncertain iconography of the Trinity in western art,[1] but the intrinsic diffi-

---

(1) contrast the subtle and convincing treatment in the picture made by Rublev for Zagorsk monastery, now in the Tetryakov museum in Moscow.

culty of the subject must be born in mind. From the time of the 'dogmatic sarcophagus' in the Lateran museum, which presents three bearded dignitaries working together on a tiny Eve while Adam sleeps, many expedients were tried until Benedict XIV wisely suppressed the practice altogether. A Louvre picture from Avignon very unhappily shows Father and Son breathing forth the Holy Spirit (enough to convince Byzantine theologians that they were right after all), while Van Eyck shows God the Father in cope and papal crown. It needed Michelangelo on the Sistine roof to produce a convincing God the Father. It would be interesting to argue for the 'Creation of Adam' there as the high moment of Christian humanism. Cajetan, commenting on St Thomas' articles on image-veneration (ST III, q.25) shrewdly suggests that you are better off with something like a dove or a hand coming from a cloud.

Art presents religion and theology in their best clothes — or what the time conceives to be their best clothes. It tends to make order out of chaos and gloss over defects. If the artist works for a patron who is an establishment man — pope, bishop, abbot or rich layman anxious to do the right thing — the patron knows what he wants and is not likely to pay if he does not get it. Hence art of this sort is not likely openly to reflect much of the sort of disquiets listed above, much less the theological troubles wracking the university of Paris. The succession of artists who adorned S Francesco in the century following the saint's death, and those who perpetuated his memory in so many other places, portrayed the Franciscan ideal as lived by the saint and his companions and told in the various lives. But it is cynical to suppose that this ideal meant nothing either to artists or patrons and survived only among the Spirituals. The artists Cimabue and Giotto would not have survived in the world of the Spirituals; yet they would not have succeeded (much less would Dante) if they had taken the official world at its own valuation. The artist *can* be a prophet within the institution. Where symbolism and allegory are accepted he may criticize or protest obliquely. If St Francis is the subject, the artist need do hardly more than present him, no longer as a legendary saint or martyr, but as one whose memory is green, an inspiration or a silent reproach; though of course the first 'contemporary' saint to take an international place in art, Thomas Becket, was an inspiration and reproach of a rather contrary sort.

More important for the future of art, he may, under this inspiration, begin to look for a fresher, less hieratic language. The humanising of Christocentric art, the greater prominence given to the maternal theme, which is paralleled in theology — at least in spiritual theology — go with the 'new style' of Giotto and with Italian simplification of Gothic forms, return to human scale, cult of light and airiness, which issued in the Tuscan renaissance. All this is quite distinguishable from a cult of the antique and still more from hankering after paganism, though these eventually came to play their part. Much ink has been spilt arguing about when and where they did so, or even trying to do away with the 'Renaissance' altogether, but the fact that you cannot fix a date for something does not prove it is not there.

High Gothic witnesses to (tries to *manifest*) a total solution of the problem of Church and society — or rather the problem of what life is all about and how it should be organized. The encyclopedias, the *Summae* were no accident: all you wanted to know could be written down or even embodied in a Church. It would be rash to say this was never an Italian ideal when two of its greatest literary exponents were Dante and Aquinas, but it was not the ideal of the shrewd, down-to-earth, politically ruthless Italian communes once they had got the Germans off their backs and felt their own strength. It is significant that Dante, with his conservative clinging to the imperial dream, spent most of his life in exile, while Aquinas seemed equally detached from Gothic Paris and Norman-Byzantine Naples.

Of course the power of Gothic sculpture could not fail to be felt, and is interestingly presented as a family tension in the work of the two greatest thirteenth-century sculptors, Nicola Pisano, the classical-minded father, and Giovanni the Gothicising son, who in fact had more influence on the renaissance sculptors than his father.

Later town Gothic in the North shows the tendency of the comprehensive Gothic vision to decline into emotional luxuriance — a kind of image-jungle not without analogies with our own. After it, to go into Brunelleschi's Pazzi chapel is like coming out into fresh, stirring air and sunshine having walked through a thick wood on a wet day. I always imagine Bramante going from Duke Frederick's court at Urbino to Milan and looking at the cathedral, saying 'we must put a stop to this'. If it is a theological process to change radically men's attitude to God and the supernatural, then art and architecture have never been more theological than they were in fourteenth and fifteenth century Italy.

Even so the later, more dogmatic humanists exaggerated the early manifestations of this, reading history backwards, as is our constant temptation. If we turn for a moment to poetry, we find that two of the first major poems in western vernacular literature, Italian and English respectively, Dante's *Divine Comedy* and Langland's *Piers Plowman* are marvellous expressions of the medieval vision of the universal order. Poetry had had a long, fluctuating relation with the Christian world-view through the medium of late classical and medieval Latin — whether celebrating with splendid economy the mysteries of the Faith in liturgical hymns and sequences from the Greek and Latin Fathers down to Jacopone's *Stabat Mater* and Aquinas' Corpus Christi office, or sighing for lost pagan delights and expressing the revolt of the average sensual man against devouring monastic discipline, or poking an irreverent tongue at the solemnities of clerical establishment rhetoric. St Francis and Jacopone had expressed their love for man and nature or their pity for the sufferings of Christ and his mother in the rather late-developing Italian vernacular, and the court poets of Frederick II (including himself), like those of Provence, had given literary forms to other kinds of love.

Dante Alighieri (1265-1321) gathers up all this and infinitely more in his *Divine Comedy*, a vision, sometimes terrifying, sometimes sublime, of man under the judgment of God. The poet's hard journey through hell and purgatory to paradise is no detached tour, but a tremendous *ascesis*, an 'ascent of the

72

mind to God', under first the *lumen naturale* (light of nature, personified by Virgil) and then the *lumen gratiae* (light of grace, Beatrice). Theology and art have rarely been so wedded, but such forbidding labels as 'the world's greatest theological (or philosophical) poet' are misleading — disastrously so if they hold back readers by suggesting a versified *Summa*. Apart from the passionate and vivid transmuting of his own life's experience (and prejudice), the heart of his total triumph is lucidity of design and of language (not the same as easiness) and his untiring genius for manifesting the difficult or the remote thing through the homely image.

But these last qualities, which link this great visionary with the Renaissance, are precisely the qualities of a poet. Dante the political theorist of the *De Monarchia* merely contrasts unfavourably with the cool, realistic political thinking of Aquinas and with the practical realism of the communes. The latter, with their anti-imperial separatism, their concern with trade, with immediate purposes, found it hard to accept the notion of a history leading from heathen darkness to the light of Christ. Indeed, as Friedrich Heer has suggested, Italian culture had been since the days of Boethius and Cassiodorus a kind of resistance-movement, a struggle to keep alive an austere but humane ideal of purity and clarity of style against even Christian influence, whether Gothic or Byzantine. (Italians went on calling Gothic 'the modern manner' down to 1500 or so.) Thus they were disposed for the kind of revival under the influences of classical models formulated by, for example, Petrarch.

Renaissance can be seen as an assertion of Italian national ideals, which has theological implications, since, instead of seeing Christianity as a fish sees the sea, it 'places' Christianity in a much wider scheme of history. This comes out very strongly in Leon Battista Alberti's two foundational works of the Florentine renaissance, his treatise on painting and his *De Re Aedificatoria*. Though, as will be seen later, he talks shrewdly about 'our religion' and its relations with art, Book VII of the architectural treatise, under the title 'How to Decorate Temples', talks about the temples of the gods and takes its examples from ancient history. Again when he tells us that 'Painting greatly advances piety, by which above all we are linked to the higher powers, and holds our minds to pure religion', and reminds us 'how much it contributes to honest delight and the beauty of things', he is talking in terms compatible with a Christian world-view but not at all dominated by it — rather seeing it as in need of deliverance from barbarism as much as anything else. This is perfectly expressed in his taking of a Gothic church in Rimini and 'encasing' it in one of his own designs, breathing the spirit of *convenienza, concinnitas, gentilezza*, reverence for geometry and all the other Tuscan Renaissance virtues. The building was less well known by its Christian dedication than as the 'Malatesta temple' after the notorious tyrant of the city who paid for it.

Michelet, in the nineteenth century, called the Renaissance 'the discovery of the world and of man', and the label was taken up by many others whose main interest in the period was, as Hauser says, 'to establish the genealogy of liberalism'. Theologically and otherwise the Renaissance was more complex and interesting.

To begin with it cannot be separated from the life of fifteenth-century Florence. This was a prosperous city skilled in trade and crafts, where however the elaborate guilds made for intimate links between religion and daily life, though the social and political occasions for expressing late medieval disquiet were many and often took hysterical religious forms as in Savonarola's time. Much Florentine building and art — the baptistery, S Miniato, the *badia* at Fiesole — had long made visible ideals which were anything but pagan but also anything but Gothic.

Giotto's interests in solidity, simplification, economy of dramatic expression, in giving depth by architectural perspective (all shared to some extent by the Lorenzettis in Siena) were already 'Renaissance' interests, though their influence remained ineffective until other factors came into play.

By contrast the Studium or university of Florence was like others the undisputed domain of the schoolmen, and of that medieval theology which was 'more ambitious than critical'.

Hence it was in literature and learning that the first signs of something revolutionary appeared. Humanist masters began to import a new study of the classics, a new philosophical method, a new vision of culture. But the real leaders were outside the university. Ficino (1433-99) translated Plato (the first complete translation into any western language) with Plotinus and other neo-platonists, and aimed to make them the centre of a new living system, but he was also a priest (at forty) and a canon of Florence aiming to harmonize his system with the Christian religion. He wanted a *docta religio*. Ambrogio Traversari, the Camaldolese monk and humanist, divided his time between translating Diogenes Laertius and studying Hebrew for the better understanding of the Scriptures. Landino wrote a commentary on Dante which became indispensable. Lorenzo the Magnificent wrote religious plays. Pico della Mirandola even aimed at a society for world peace. The 'academies' of Florence, bringing together churchmen with poets, doctors, jurists, musicians, scholars and artists for good conversation, were 'devout fraternities', and, for all the pagan affectations with which they began, in their mature development they aimed not at returning to the past but at purifying Christian learning. Revival of Greek and purification of Latin were aimed at (as well as the study of Hebrew), but, as Poliziano said to a critic, 'You say that after studying Cicero for so long I still do not express myself like Cicero. But I am not Cicero, and it is precisely by studying him that I have learned to be myself'.[2]

The great Florentines, Brunelleschi, Donatello, Ghiberti, were all enthusiasts for the antique but not imitators of it in the sense of copiers, except for exercise. Painters loved to set their scenes against classical backgrounds, but their figures were dressed in the fashion of the day. It was just for this reason that the return to the classical was an invigorating and liberating thing in earlier fifteenth-century Florence — it was not allowed to dominate and deaden.

---

(2) Quoted in G. Martinelli (ed.), *The World of Renaissance Florence* (Macdonald 1968), p. 159.

This is true for artists during the Tuscan Renaissance. Can we say that the Florentine neo-platonism which recent art-historians have seen as so profoundly affecting art from the late fifteenth century onwards was (as we have seen it claimed to be) a purification of Christian learning? The Thomist and the present-day anti-metaphysician might well come together to doubt this. If Aquinas' philosophy was one of distinctions, Ficino's was one of fusion, if not confusion. One reason why Ficino's system (if this is the right word) was important for art and attractive to 'art-lovers' (though it interested only very few artists), was that, in an elaborate ontological structure, it gave much greater prominence to 'beauty', identifying it with the good. Aquinas had defined beauty in a phenomenological way — *integritas*, *consonantia* (proportion), *claritas*. For Ficino it is 'the splendour of the face of God' called beauty insofar as it begins in God and attracts to him, *amor divinus* (divine love) insofar as it passes into the world and ravishes it, and beatitude insofar as it reverts to the creator. Earthly existence is at best a kind of imprisonment, like living below the surface of water, but beauty accessible to the senses, especially to hearing and sight, can raise men to enraptured contemplation of that which transcends not only perception but reason.

Those who can thus rise up to the intelligible world can there apprehend the truth directly, in a flash, without the need of words and arguments, discursive speech, those crutches which can and will be discarded in the realm of ideas, the realm of pure spirit to which the poet, the seer and the lover can aspire. As Plotinus had said long before, 'It must not be thought that in the intelligible world the gods and the blessed see propositions; everything expressed there is a beautiful image.'

There is a conception of the artists' function and power which goes far beyond the rather pragmatic conceptions of 'visual aids', sometimes read into medieval art — though it is a conception we find already foreshadowed, for example in Suger of St Denis (cf. Ch. 5, p. 66). It is in the end decisive in transforming the medieval craftsman into the 'genius', melancholy, withdrawn, full of 'divine' frenzy and giving currency in art-discourse to such terms as inspiration and creation. (The latter is still being studiously avoided by Leonardo, but has established itself by the sixteenth century.) Painting, architecture, music are raised to the venerable company of the 'liberal' arts.

But all this happens in a setting in which religious demands are still bringing the artist most of his patronage. The artist's developing claim to see beyond the dross of matter and to apprehend that Beauty that dwells in the intelligible world, far from invoking any immediate claims to the autonomy of art, is only seen as valid in a theological context. Where Plato had despised the painters of his time as tricksters, the Renaissance platonists saw the figurative artist, not just as providing an illiterate's Bible, but as the ally of rare spirits in their reaching-up to the divine.

Plato's higher world did not want to be known by the lower, but Christian theology is one of divine condescension in the true original sense. Scripture, history, creation are revelatory of God, who in his mercy gives symbolic value to everything. The pelican is more than a metaphor for the charity of Christ which we have hit upon: God himself prefigures his love in the habits of the pelican.

Florentine neo-platonism had the weaknesses of a fashionable cult and was full of esoteric and hermetic extravagances, but here we see the seed of a rich, if ambiguous, side of the Counter-Reformation which owes the minimum to the Council of Trent and to the pragmatic churchman's notion of 'harnessing the artist to the mission of the Church'[3] (cf. p. 88).

A masterly re-interpretation (or recovery of a true interpretation) by E. H. Gombrich of Raphael's decoration of the Vatican Stanza della Segnatura has shown how Renaissance secularising accounts of these frescoes were based, not only on secularist prejudice, but on failure to attend to the scheme as a whole, often due to working from prints or photographs.

---

(3) E.H. Gombrich, *Symbolic Images* (Phaidon Press 1972), pp. 85ff.

Raphael and his theological advisers were not concerned to propound revolutionary ideas but to illustrate the commonplaces of the time — that the dignity of all knowledge is derived from its link with the divine, that all intellectual disciplines somehow partake of the revelation of higher truth. The aim was not to profane the sacred but to sanctify the profane. The respect paid to ancient poetry and philosophy could only enhance the importance of *divinarum rerum notitia* (knowledge of divine things) . . . (the real title of the misnamed *disputa del sacramento*).

This is the optimism of the high Renaissance expressed by one who did not outlive it, as Michelangelo and Titian, for example, did; an optimism about reconciling the revived classical tradition with the Christian tradition. To the earlier Renaissance the problem hardly presented itself explicitly. This often made for what now seem gross inconsistencies. For example, Alberti could write like a modern liturgical reformer:

> When our religion began, our ancestors, upright men, used to meet for a supper together, not to stuff themselves with food, but to become more gentle by this fellowship and to go home full of good counsel and eager for virtue. When they had tasted rather than consumed the prepared feast, there was a reading and a sermon on theological themes and the soul of each burned with desire to act for the good of all and to cultivate virtue. (Then they gave alms according to their means. . .) When the emperors allowed all this to be done publicly there was little deviation from original customs. There was only one altar. . . at which the faithful gathered, and they celebrated one sacrifice a day.
>
> Then came the times which every serious person should blame. Bishops show themselves rarely but have crammed churches with altars, the noblest things lose value for excess of availability.

Yet he could also design a church as a monument to a tyrant's mistress, which the humanist pope Pius II (admittedly in the middle of a political quarrel with the tyrant) described as 'so rich in pagan works as to represent a place for worshippers of the devil rather than a Christian temple'. Donatello could make a great Christian-classical tragedy out of the entombment of Christ, a superb yet horrifying piece of expressionism out of the aged Mary Magdalene, an ambiguous rout out of the capers of cherubs in a choir gallery.

Yet in the end what counts and endures most in the fifteenth-century revolution of vision and technique — the mastery of perspective and proportion, the ordering of objects in space, the gravity and nobility, the certainty and splendour in the works of Masaccio, Fra Angelico and Piero della Francesca, of Ghiberti and Donatello, has little to do with neo-platonism, much more with the vigour of the Tuscan mind. To see a church like S Maria della Consolazione at Todi or S Biagio at Montepulciano in its serene setting, to enter and feel the satisfaction of these perfect relations, space articulated in golden stone, is to feel that man, enlarging his own imaginative grasp, has found new ways of directing himself to God.

This sense of a magic new world which is yet an enlargement of the Christian world, an artist's vision which is an enlargement of theological vision, is nowhere stronger than in the work of perhaps the greatest fifteenth-century painter, Piero della Francesca. Antiquarian enthusiasm, scientific curiosity, none of the humanist virtues begins to make sense of his work apart from the central Christian convictions which he grasped with the unique intensity of genius. As Lord Clark has put it, 'Two unconscious beliefs direct his imagination, his belief in the continuity of life and the nearness of God.(4) Elsewhere the marriage of Christianity and classicism was to prove a stormy one leading to plentiful offspring but also to strain and at last coldness. In Piero they come together in grave, assured harmony. Looking at the Christ who rises from the tomb in that shabby little town hall of Borgo San Sepolcro, we feel like quoting Plotinus to the theologian. 'It must not be thought that in the intelligible world the gods and the blessed see propositions, everything expressed there is a beautiful image'.

---

(4) Kenneth Clark, *Piero della Francesca* (Phaidon Press 1951), p. 54.

COUNTER-REFORMATION AND BAROQUE

St Stephen enraged the Sanhedrin by telling them, 'the Most High does not dwell in houses made with hands', and citing Isaiah: 'Heaven is my throne and earth is my footstool. What house will you build for me, says the Lord, or what is the place of my rest?' (Acts 7. 48-9). This view continued to be held by some in the Church while others favoured building Jerusalem on earth with stone. The dispute over the building of the huge hillside church to house St Francis's bones reflected this tension as well as the wider one about the future of the order. Nicholas V at the outset of the Renaissance came down firmly for the second view, and first entertained the idea of rebuilding St Peter's:

> To create solid and stable convictions in the minds of the uncultured masses, there must be something that appeals to the eye: a proper faith, sustained only on doctrines, will never be anything but feeble and vacillating; but if the authority of the Holy See were visibly displayed in majestic buildings, imperishable memorials and witnesses seemingly planted by the hand of God himself, belief would grow and strengthen. . . Noble edifices combining taste and beauty with imposing proportions would immensely conduce to the exaltation of the Chair of St Peter.[1]

This, though not necessarily with such emphasis on the Papacy, was to be the manifesto of one school of thought till long after the time when Church art had ceased to offer much that was original and significant. Yet though St Bernardine, Nicholas of Cusa, St Antoninus and most fiercely Savonarola denounced Renaissance art from the other standpoint, little early Renaissance art is open to the charge of ostentation or

---

(1) Quoted in J. Lees-Milne, *St. Peter's* (Hamish Hamilton 1967), p. 124.

lavishness. The soft grey stone which articulated the white walls of Brunelleschi's churches was well called *pietra serena;* he drew his effects from restraint, luminous simplicity, perfect shapes and proportions, human scale. The Augustinian school understood and approved this. The circular plan, which the conservative saw as pagan (having come to accept that accident of history, the basilica as having some almost doctrinal sanction), could be argued for on liturgical grounds, and was to be important down to the end of the baroque period. Renaissance theorists took the Christian adaptation of the classical elements seriously — Serlio explained how the Doric order was suitable for churches dedicated to Christ and to male saints, the Ionic to matrons and widows, the Corinthian for our Lady and virgin saints and for the building of convents.

The use of the new forms on a colossal scale is inseparably connected with the brief High Renaissance in Rome and with the decision of the dynamic Julius II to grasp the nettle and pull down old St Peter's. This was bound to strike many as terrifying impiety, but Alberti fifty years earlier had condemned the building as dangerous, pointing out that the south wall was six feet out of the perpendicular. Bramante's ruthlessness and ambition (he was an old man in a hurry) underlined the iconoclasm, but his new design was a bold and splendid invention, and the four giant piers he began to build to support the dome have remained the pivot of all subsequent schemes and developments.

Artistically the building, which reflects the pattern of a unique century and a half in the history of genius, had a mixed and in some points unhappy history, but from the beginning under Julius II to the enthronement of the supposed chair of Peter by Bernini, under Alexander VII in 1666, a single theological theme consistently dominated the work — the glorification of the Petrine office and primacy and of the historical papacy. In its achieved form it can easily strike the casual visitor as a single-minded essay in triumphalism, but in fact it reflects three or four great and different phases of artistic thinking and taste closely related to some very turbulent religious history. It will be a necessary point of reference at a number of stages in the rest of this essay.

The High Renaissance was a brief flowering, cruelly cut off by the sack of Rome in 1527 and by the outbreak of the Protestant revolt. We might be tempted to symbolise it in the abortive history of Julius II's tomb. Certainly a generation of Romans got used to the frustrating sight of a half-demolished St Peter's standing beside what Bramante had begun. Yet with the Counter-Reformation and Trent a new vigour appears; the glorification of the Petrine office is intensified, if in a rather shriller, more defensive key. Over the whole range of religious art serenity, briefly achieved, is lost. The insecurity, the panic of churchmen reflects itself for much of the sixteenth-century in ill-conceived attempts at regulation: the positive, creative forces of the Counter-Reformation do not emerge with new serenity until the Baroque period, by which time there has been some loss, some distortion.

But this is to look ahead. One personality bestrides the transitional period, Michelangelo. No categories contain him, yet no one escaped his influence. It is not easy to say how far his unquiet spirit reflects the religious spirit of his age and how far it contributes to creating it. He had the power of genius to assimilate and transmute neo-platonic thought, the regained experience of classical sculpture, Flemish pathos. His St Peter's Pietá is a rare moment of fusion, of harmony between Christian and classical. He was to revert to the theme again, in his last years, in a very different, more personal spirit. Renaissance artists were as serious about the 'Christian interpretation' of the nude body as about that of any classical form. Most of them went far beyond the classical range in exploiting it to express the spiritual, but none ventured so far as Michelangelo.

Medieval art had used the nude mainly to express tragedy or humiliation — the fall of Adam and Eve, the crucifixion (with natural indecisiveness), martyrdoms, the damned in the Last Judgment. Clothes of variety and splendour were a medieval mode and symbol of exaltation; the Gothic nude, which looks *deprived* of clothes, could not be. The brief period in which Vitruvian man was indeed the measure of all things, in which the classical nude, based on repose and balance, physical health and perfection was seen confidently and serenely as a vehicle of spiritual expression is a short one — as short as the period of balance and harmony between classical and Christian which is the High Renaissance. Events of religious history and general theological anxieties did much to destroy this security and balance, but hardly as much as Michelangelo's own spiritual and artistic odyssey.

The high seriousness of the Renaissance, the heroic ideal, the contempt for decorative triviality, of Piero, Mantegna, Donatello — these possessed him, and he brought them to their summit in works like David and Moses and, above all, in the Sistine ceiling. These pictures of creation culminating in the transfusion of divine life into man, and pointing forward to the Christian recreation, are surely the high-water mark of visual theological statement, beside which all words but those of Genesis are pedestrian; and their medium of utterance is the human body made heroic. When it was finished, and the plastic arts raised to a new plane of significance, Rome had still a dozen or more golden years to run before the Sack, rather less before the first rumblings of the Protestant movement. But for the cramped and exhausted painter the Renaissance was already over. He had grasped intuitively the ultimate incompatibility of Christianity and classicism. He was first a sculptor, who believed only in the *via di levare*, the wrenching of the Idea out of the rock, the *pietra dura ed alpestre*, which reflected the struggle to deliver his own spirit from the shackles of the flesh, the tyranny of the senses. His classicism and his neo-platonism were haunted by Savonarola. The last fifty years of his work were dominated by the themes of crucifixion, death, judgment. Even the architectural might (fundamentally sculptural) by which, at the bidding of the Counter-Reformation pope Paul III, he pulled the design of St Peter's into an uneasy unity, was put forth only because he believed God had thrust the task on him.

The powerful yet languid figures on the tombs of Julius II (which even at its most grandiose was never intended as a triumphal monument of the pagan type but as a deeply Christian essay on death) and of the Medici, the tortured bodies of the Last Judgment are thus interpreted by Morey:

> Michelangelo's powerful inhibited figures reflect the disparity between Christian emotion and the antique ideal, free human will and the will of God: the rational forms of classic sculpture were not made for the ecstasy of a Christian mystic, they writhe in the possession of an unfamiliar spirit and betray by brutal distortion, incongruous proportions and discordant composition the force of the collision of medieval Christianity with the Renaissance.(2)

Does this apply even to Christ the Judge on the Sistine wall? This is Michelangelo's most startling departure from traditional iconography, from the Byzantine Pantocrators and gaunt medieval Judges. It is the most daring and direct attempt to Christianise the Renaissance hero. It may well have convinced him that along that road was no more progress. His drawings of the Resurrection show stages in the refining away of mere physical power and attraction; his late drawings of the crucifixion renounce much of the stress and distortion Morey refers to; while in the last Pietás everything that could suggest the god-like proportions and energy of man, the measure of all things, has gone, and there is nothing but the consummate expression, almost beyond technique, of the great spirit — as in the last work of Shakespeare and Beethoven. But this was not the point at which Michelangelo's imitators took him up. Most of the artists who enlisted in the service of the Counter-Reformation were obsessed rather with the cartoons of the Last Judgment.

1520, the year in which Raphael died, Luther was excommunicated and Michelangelo began planning the Medici funeral chapel, is usually assigned rather over-precisely as the end of the High Renaissance: art down to the end of the sixteenth century is labelled 'Mannerist'. The label covers a mixed group

---

(2) C. R. Morey, *Christian Art*, quoted in E. Panofsky, *Studies in Iconology* (New York, Harper & Row, 1972), p. 177.

of elements. There is a breaking up of the classical harmony and repose of the Renaissance and especially of the unity and logical coherence of space which (in painting) landscape, architecture and even clouds had been induced to serve. In buildings too, architectural elements came to be used in odd and strained ways. In sculpture, it is the writhing limbs of the Laocoon rather than the classical Greek models that are emulated. All those elements can be found in Michelangelo, but they express the struggle of a titanic mind and are transmuted by a titanic genius. In lesser artists they can decline into cleverness, feverish virtuosity, or an intellectual fashion which is consciously deforming, abstruse or even bizarre; or into an epicurean cult of subtlety and elegance. When chaos threatens to overwhelm, the tendency is to fall back on *recent* tradition — that is, the 'classicism' of the Renaissance without its freshness.

This blanket pejorative account will not of course do for eighty years of intense activity which includes, for example, Titian, Tintoretto and much of El Greco. It is more helpful and more to our present purpose to look at what lay behind the stylistic changes — at that history which has suffered peculiarly from three kinds of triumphalist distortion, Catholic, Protestant and humanist, but which is now better seen for the complex thing it was.

High Renaissance vision and poise had no very deep or broad moral or intellectual foundations and was ill-equipped to survive the political, social and religious upheaval that overtook it. Yet artists and poets were sensitive to the signs of the times as they had rarely been before. The first response to the Reformation upheaval — attempt at reform in a humanist and reconciling spirit, that which ended with Contarini's failure at the Diet of Ratisbon in 1541, was a response in which Michelangelo and other artists shared. One of them, Francisco de Hollanda, has left an account (1539) of the meetings in Rome of the Oratory of Divine Love which attracted such spirits, who sat and listened while a theologian read St Paul to them. Deep spiritual disquiet and dissatisfaction was felt and reflected by artists, as it had been by Langland and Chaucer, Boccaccio and Botticelli.

The failure to come to terms with the Protestants was followed by a repressive phase, inquisition, censorship, and more haltingly by the theological and reforming programme of Trent.

Yet Trent does not utter about art until its twenty-fifth session, near the end of its eighteen years of history (1563), and when the decree comes it seems aimed mainly at the extravagances of current Mannerism. It forbids images that reflect erroneous doctrine or can lead the simple astray. Artists are to avoid opening the way to impurity by giving images provocative qualities. They are to avoid the outlandish, the unusual.

There is something of official conservatism and prudery here — already in 1559 Paul IV had ordered chemises to be painted on figures in Michelangelo's Last Judgment; Pius V did the same, and Clement VIII was only just dissuaded from painting it out altogether. But the Tridentine decree reflects a less simple-minded attitude. Its very existence is an acknowledgement of the close link between theology and the arts. It recognises too that Renaissance and Mannerist art was largely a minority cult and that recent iconography was often obscure and ambiguous. It ends by insisting on episcopal approval for all images in churches — even in those of religious houses normally exempt from diocesan control.

It was an age of crisis, which brought a call for discipline and austerity. The austerity was much reflected in sixteenth-century church building, though later Baroque additions can easily obscure this. The discipline, the desire to control art (vaguely thought of as paganising) by legislation and even by sanctions, appealed to a certain type of mind. But a broader humanist spirit had also made its way deeply among churchmen — the spirit which was alienated from the reformers by their savage iconoclasm, continued to see the arts as the natural ally of the Christian teacher, and patronized artists.

The tension is illustrated in the story of Paul Veronese, a sumptuous Venetian who painted vast biblical scenes full of overdressed women, pet dogs, drunkards and other worldly objects. Summoned before the Inquisition for one of these excesses, he said in effect, 'What about Michelangelo's nudes?'; and the Inquisitor answered, 'Don't you know that in Michelangelo's figures there is nothing that is not spiritual?'

The decisive turn was taken by the Jesuits. Ignatius, a soldier who even late in life was ready to prepare to be a religious founder and reformer by hard work in various universities, yet saw the need to cut through the theological thickets and go back to the heart of the Christian matter, which is to contemplate Christ. The *Exercises* invite us to meditate on the Gospel more in the manner of the artist than of the academic theologian; many chapters begin with the words 'Picture to yourself . . .'. Gerson, one of those acute fifteenth-century critics who if listened to might have forestalled much sixteenth-century disaster, had rejected a theological research cut off from spiritual life and accessible only to a theological elite. In the sixteenth-century religious art was in danger of following the same path. The Jesuits forced it into another more profitable one, which proved to have its own dangers.

They saw it as they saw the theatre, as an instrument of teaching, of apologetics to combat heresy, sometimes by loudly emphasising the Catholic beliefs and practices questioned by the reformers (including the use of art itself), but also by deepening the spiritual life not only of an elite but of mass congregations. The bulk of Roman High Renaissance art was physically accessible only to an elite, but a picture like Titian's glowing Assumption in a great Franciscan preaching church in Venice, by an 'olympian' Renaissance genius who was nevertheless a peasant, showed the popular possibilities of painting as early as 1518.

But these were not to be realised by schoolmasterly supervision of the new type of artist. In the immediate post-Tridentine phase a series of treatises by clerics show confusion of aim only slowly clearing. De Gilio's significantly titled *Dialogue on the Errors of Painters* (1564), as well as the indispensable insistence on loin-cloths, criticizes Michelangelo's Last Judgement for a beardless Christ — for borrowing Charon's ferry from pagan mythology, for saints who gesture like people at a bullfight, for angels grouped otherwise than laid down in the book of Revelation.

Before the end of the century half-a-dozen works had appeared, aimed at rationalising and disciplining Counter-Reformation art. No doubt they had as limited an effect as such things normally have, especially in Italy, and rigorists were soon complaining of lax application of the 'rules'. This was just as well: artists who were getting more and more secular commissions for mythological and other subjects would have been alienated, and religious art would have been driven into sanctimonious isolation much earlier than it was. As it was, mediocre painters like Vasari professed themselves glad of theological tutelage, but a genius of the highest order like Titian, the familiar of emperors and princes, could paint Venuses and Bacchanals with marvellous gusto, yet turn again in the bold free style of his last years to profound religious works. To compare his last Pieta, left unfinished at his death in 1576, with the Louvre version of the Entombment of Christ (1525) is to see how a great spirit responded to the religious renewal of the age with a depth found in the great mystics but in few theological writers, and certainly owing nothing to clerical handbooks on sacred art.

A religious revival is authentic to the extent that the permanent truths are not just 'plugged' but seen and stated afresh. This has little to do with a straining after novelty and effect, as too many sixteenth-century painters thought it had. Once or twice in history artists have been given a commission comprehensive enough to be an opportunity for a new vision of the Gospel. Giotto's Padua frescoes are an example. Sixteenth-century Venice offers another — Tintoretto's decoration of the Scuola di San Rocco. Tintoretto was a stay-at-home painter, largely self-taught though a great assimilator, no intellectual in the conventional sense. He worked for the rich medieval guild for thirty years. He was indifferent to money and honours but inwardly driven to work feverishly. The Scuola has two great halls and one smaller. Tintoretto supplied pictures for all the walls and one of the great ceilings, almost pressing them upon the guild. There are scenes from the New Testament with Old Testament parallels, and a climax in the smaller hall with three scenes of the Passion.

Tintoretto sees everything afresh and commands rich resources to express his vision: Venetian mastery of colour, a sense of the dramatic possibilities of the human form, of surprising viewpoints and foreshortening derived from Michelangelo, a treatment of light and a way of composing in diagonals which is his own. Equally the resources create the vision. The light unifies the whole experience — makes consistent the unearthliness and the exact observation of earthy detail. A huge, bold scheme is carried through coherently, though the variety is as rich as life. It is the intellect working at the tip of the senses, in Eliot's phrase. A morning spent in the small room with the scenes of the Passion is on the level of listening to Bach's St Matthew.

Tintoretto is sometimes called the greatest Counter-Reformation artist, but many elements of the Counter-Reformation thinking are lacking here. There is no concern with the Church, with glorification, with triumph over heresy. The Assumption is portrayed, but otherwise our Lady's place retains the proportions given by Scripture. St Roch is prominent on the ceiling (it was the picture painted to secure the commission), but the only other two saints, Magdalene and St Mary of Egypt, are excuses for two poems of contemplation in superb dreamy landscapes.

The Venetian guild left the painter more freedom than a Roman church or a prince might have done at that moment but it was not abused, and the cleric who complained that our Lady was not *standing* at the foot of the cross remembered his Gospel but was otherwise little equipped to look at the pictures.

On the other hand the pictures are a strong counter to the extreme Protestant denial of the power of images to put the believer in contact with the transcendent. The reforming view was that the means given by God were sufficient for this: the word was primary, and gave a pure relationship with the one

Mediator. The multiplication of images was only the consequence of a long tradition of inadequate preaching. Speech is
more 'prophetic', in being freer, more mobile, more open to
correction. This at least was the argument in its more
conscious and moderate form.

The mainstream of Counter-Reformation iconography was
a more direct challenge to all this than Tintoretto's (or El
Greco's in Spain). A new rapid advance in the building of St
Peter's under Sixtus V (1585-90), the completion of the dome,
that statement of celestial and pontifical might, the successful
transfer of the obelisk to the front of the church to symbolize
the triumph of true faith over heresy, paganism and super-
stition — these all reflected a revival of confidence as the
century drew to a close. Out of this revival grew the baroque.
The family chapel of the Roman-born Pope Paul V in St Mary
Major is a manifesto of the new programme. The iconoclast
emperors Copronymos and Leo the Armenian are shown
coming to bad ends: Heraclius, who exalted the True Cross,
and John Damascene, the theological champion of images, are
glorified. At the same time our Lady appears as the victor over
heresy, treading on a serpent of false doctrine.

From this platform was launched a campaign to hammer at
the doctrines attacked by the reformers. Our Lady is associated with the Trinity at the Creation or even before (Ara
Coeli). The supernatural virtue of St Peter's shadow is illustrated. Papal triumphs like Canossa or the quelling of Attila are
dramatised. Sacramental iconography is given a strong anti-
reform turn. Famous penitents, David, Magdalene, Peter in
tears, symbolise confession, while later John Nepomuk, who
gave his life for the confessional seal in 1383, was resurrected
from obscurity by the Jesuits and canonised in 1729, stands
with biretta, frilly cotta and crucifix on nearly every stone
bridge in South Germany. In Last Suppers there is a switch
from the betrayal motif to the consecration or communion,
and last communions — St Jerome, St Francis, the miraculous
one of St Catherine of Siena — become popular. So do saints
who were prominent for good works — Elizabeth of Hungary,
Hedwig, John of God, Charles Borromeo. The heroic ideal of

martyrdom, preached and practised by the Jesuits, receives dramatic, sometimes gruesome treatment.

Obsession with transience and death was part of the sixteenth-century malaise (and went on longer). Donne, Shakespeare, Webster and others had it in England. It had its effect on the figurative arts with their symbols, but still more did the Jesuit preachers' elaborations of the meditations on death from the *Exercises* multiply skulls and skeletons. The belligerence and triumphalism in Counter-Reformation art was offset by an intense concern for individual salvation. The tension between the two is evident in the poetry and life of the neurotic Tasso.

Counter-Reformation art, as it moves to its climax in the baroque, gains something in understanding by being related to the curious history of the Jesuit drama. From insignificant beginnings in the early colleges in mid-sixteenth century there grew, as the Society advanced in numbers, prestige and influence, a vast international corpus of didactic apologetic plays on biblical, classical and moral themes. They were spectacles rather than literary masterpieces, appealing to the eye more than the ear, but their success as a pedagogical instrument carried them from the school to the market-place and eventually to the spacious Jesuit churches. The emphasis here too is on the bellicose aspects of Bible and theology, but the essential battle remains that which concerns the retreat-father — the battle for the human soul.

The comparison illuminates one side of baroque art, but only one of many sides. The resolution of spiritual tensions and the release of spiritual energy at the beginning of the seventeenth century was intimately bound up with successful resolutions, for example, of architectural problems. The spirit of Counter-Reformation architecture, like that of the thirteenth-century friars' churches, was more utilitarian than is often realised. A spacious interior and an imposing facade for a busy street were the main requirements. (The Gesu, commonly spoken of as a baroque 'prototype', acquired its rich crust much later). Juggling the elements of the classical orders into a two-storey front to cover nave and aisles was usually a rather flat and tentative business in the sixteenth-century. The achievement of Carlo Maderna at S Susanna in Rome (1603) marks a new stage of concentration and depth, and in the next fifty years the plasticity and inventiveness achieved by Pietro da Cortona, Carlo Rainaldi, Bernini and above all Borromini, culminated in such marvels as St Carlino and St Ivo, where stone seems to be bent like plasticine to achieve striking effect. The contrast may be illustrated at one glance by comparing the front of the Oratorian Chiesa Nuova in Rome with Borromini's next door.

The scope for exploiting light and movement, intersecting planes, solid and space was even greater in interiors, and here the talents of the painter, the sculptor, the stucco-worker were brought to bear on a total effect, a kind of perilous harmony in which the whole is very much more than the sometimes pedestrian parts. At its best the baroque church is a unity of architecture and decoration conspiring to astonish and excite, to draw the emotions upward and heavenward. This aim links it with the Gothic rather than the classical style (though the means used differ greatly) and does something to explain the later successful advances of the style in German-speaking lands. Both Gothic and baroque are dynamic rather than static; to express movement, energy, drive is their purpose, and all in the cause of faith and recovered confidence. Yet with all their sophistication of planning and modelling and their conscious departure from renaissance 'modules', the great seventeenth-century Romans retained a firm grasp of classical principles and their 'theatricality' often covers brilliant solutions of practical problems, achieved with assurance and lightness.

The theology of baroque is a theology of glory, even of ecstasy. In 1622 four great Counter-Reformation saints were canonised on the same day — Teresa of Avila, Philip Neri, Ignatius of Loyola and Francis Xavier. Three of the four had been visionaries. The tableaux prepared for the canonisation ceremonies not only added to iconography but changed it. Bernini's masterpiece of St. Teresa's 'Transverberation' in Rome uses all the resources of a very great sculptor to bring mystical experience out of the private chamber or the inner recesses of the soul into the theatre. Family parties stand in boxes commenting animatedly on the saint's transports. She and her loving surrender are the proud possession of the church, vividly grasped. This olympian work was to have a long, numerous and very mixed progeny. Its influence was powerful enough to replace, for example, Giotto's in Franciscan iconography, it quickly affected pictures of such saints as Magdalene, Paul, Cecilia (whose body had been brought to light in 1599) and later, in the great German baroque monasteries, such an unlikely figure as Benedict. But the baroque aspired to do much more than make the faithful spectators of the ecstasies of the saints. It aimed to draw them into heaven, and we can trace this from its beginning in illusionist painting to the climax in which architectural design itself seems to escape the confines of walls. But dome had symbolised heaven and the infinite since the Byzantine architects first solved its structural problems. The more ambitious domes of the sixteenth century added realism to symbol. Correggio, who died as early as 1534, was the pioneer at Parma of ecstatic crowd-painting in upward perspective partly learned from Mantegna, which filled domes and curved ceilings with the illusion of the sky, and was to become a staple of baroque and rococo interiors. Dome and ceiling thus become less a covering for a church than a gateway to a celestial kingdom.

The seventeenth century Jesuit lay-brother Andrea Pozzo perfected this as an element of baroque, with his extraordinary command of perspective-painting of architecture, though it is perhaps to eighteenth-century Germany, with the lighter colour-harmonies inherited from Tiepolo, that its greatest achievements belong. The constricting classical space is thrown open and what the daring builders of the choir at Beauvais had tried to do in stone is surpassed by illusion. The Jesuits had much to do with internationalising the baroque style and maintaining the Counter-Reforming impulse. It succeeded most and was prolonged down to mid-eighteenth century in those countries where the Counter-Reformation was most successful. It was the influence of the most imaginative of great Italians, Borromini and Guarini, that was the strongest medium of exportation. But the South Germans especially added their own distinctive contribution. The true German rococo, which is architecture, not mere decoration, the work, that is, of Zimmermann and Neumann, deserves the name of a separate style, because it used structural and architectonic as well as decorative devices to carry the dematerialisation of the church to its furthest point. Vierzehnheiligen, Steinhausen, Die Wies and the rest can be thought of as *theatrum sacrum*, a staging of the *ecclesia triumphans*, but it is a world to which the worshipper is transposed, not one he is looking at through a proscenium. It is no mere matter of *trompe d'oeil*, stucco draperies and angels perilously poised on cornices blurring the bounds between real and fictitious space (though the characteristic *rocaille* decoration greatly increased this); the enclosing walls themselves seem to be dissolved by intricacies of lighting and arcading. There is no verbal or photographic substitute for the experience of such a building — which is essentially an experience of movement, like music, and an experience which, by abolishing the confines of time and space, creates a supra-mundane world in which visual theology, the vast scenes of the Redemption or of Christian history, unfold not as past but as immanent present into which the onlooker is drawn. A preacher at Diessen (one of the great Bavarian churches of the style) put it briefly: 'the church is heaven'.

It is curious that the commonest term of criticism of this Church art (as of the music which went with it) in the northern Protestant-Puritan tradition absorbed by most northern Catholics, is 'worldly'. (Perhaps one should say *was*, since there is now a growing appreciation of baroque). Never perhaps in history has brilliant teamwork so combined to create in one building the illusion of *another* world.

The transmutation was more than merely sensuous — the seeming riot of colour and writhing shapes is governed by a complex allegory and symbolism drawing on the biblical resources and those of traditional iconography, but greatly expanding them and weaving new combinations. Such seeming exercises in extravagance as the pulpits of Zwiefalten and Die Wies are in fact lyrical theological essays, the one portraying the pentecostal storm accompanying the Holy Spirit, the other combining the theme of the complex relationship of sin and death with Ezekiel's vision of the valley of bones. The modern visitor needs sharp eyes, good neck-muscles and either encyclopaedic learning or a first-rate guide to take in fully one of these churches.

How many of those for whom they were built could take them in? The short answer no doubt is that the ensemble operated on more than one level, like a Shakespeare play or a work of Bach, but it is dangerous to divide one level too sharply from another. The social background to baroque and rococo art is surprisingly varied. Princely patronage, ecclesiastical or secular, played a great part, but so did popular piety and village crafts. There were no doubt few Urban VIII's, who, when asked the moral significance of Bernini's Daphne Laureola, immediately improvised a couple of Latin hexameters to express it, yet Bernini was essentially a great popular artist and a versatile one, who worked much in all branches of the theatre, including writing.

The seventeenth-century papacy celebrated (in building and embellishment) the saving of much of Europe for Catholicism and the extension of its sway into the new continents. The German princes after the terrible Thirty Years' War celebrated peace and recovery after the pattern set at Versailles. Religious celebration was one side of the medal. The great German monasteries inspired by the Escorial — Melk, Weingarten, S Florian, Einsiedeln, Klosterneuberg — were no doubt the product of what contemporaries called the *Bauwurm*, the building bug, and had little to do with the original monastic ideal; yet they expressed a powerful contemporary ideal of religious society and culture and they have added much to our civilised and scholarly heritage — in this respect we can say that in the capitalist democracies of the past century much more money has been spent on ostentatious church-building to far less purpose.

But princely display does not account for all German

baroque and rococo — in fact it accounts for few of the best examples. These are pilgrimage-churches, standing in meadows or on hill-sides, by architects who rose to immortality from unlikely beginnings as local plasterers or masons, or monastic novices or lay-brothers. The success, the overwhelming impact of such churches, comes from their being planned by team-work as a single whole of architecture and decoration, into which went a vast amount of theological thinking and consul-tation. What they still mean to the people of Austria and South Germany can be seen by anybody who goes there on Sunday or a feast-day.

To insist on the teamwork of local craftsmen is not to leave baroque explicable as naive showmanship. Bernini and Rubens, on whom we have no space to dwell, are baroque geniuses who have the seriousness of religion as well as of great art, while the habit of thinking of the eighteenth century as the age of reason can make us surprised that during the first half of it the very greatest art was still religious. Yet as Pevsner wrote thirty years ago (what was certainly true then though perhaps no longer), 'No church designed after 1760 is among the his-torically leading examples of architecture'.

ALIENATION AND DECLINE

There are several explanations of the sudden decline. The historian points out that rococo village churches went on being built in Bavaria until in October 1770 the Prince Elector forbade all freedom of planning and profile, all 'laughable' ornament, and insisted on 'noble simplicity'. This was done of course in the name of enlightenment and neo-classicism, and a few years later in the same spirit the Archbishop of Salzburg was legislating against everything from Mozart to Christmas cribs. In this sense the baroque world fell by the very force of Church-state absolutism by which in part it had risen.

But neither enlightenment nor neo-classicism were simply new fashions appearing from nowhere. They cannot be understood apart from doubts and antipathies as old as baroque itself, which reflect its weaknesses.[1] These doubts and antipathies were by no means confined to Protestants — they were well marked in France, where superficially the result of the Reformation battles was most completely a Catholic triumph. It marks the pervasive strength of baroque that it constantly weighed heavily on French art, which as constantly resisted it, but baroque was compounded of many elements, and it was the classical strands in the Italian inheritance that dominated in France. In the age of Louis XIV the triumph of Catholicism was taken up into the triumph of the French monarchy, and art and architecture were part of a vast civil service organised to maintain and celebrate absolutism. The French preference for classical grandeur and formalism reinforced and was reinforced by this. The Sorbonne and the

---

(1) In his last masterpiece at Neresheim (recently superbly restored) Balthasar Neumann abandoned rocaille, and intended to have no ornament apart from a few paintings; the rather incongruous neo-classical decor of gilded urns, etc. was added after his death.

Invalides reveal Baroque concerns and skills to the architect's eye, but the general effect has little relation with Roman baroque and still less with that of South Germany or even Austria, where the political-religious concern was superficially similar. The religion which triumphs here is Gallican; this is the proper setting for Bossuet's sermons. Poussin, though he spent most of his life in Rome, more obviously resists the unclassical elements in Baroque with his statuesque sacred scenes.

But there was a deeper, more theological resistance to the grandiose allurements of the holy kingdom of Versailles. Even Bossuet saw the hollowness and unrighteousness of it and said so; but he spoke of blots and scars on what he basically accepted as the true order. Rigaud's portrait of him tells us almost as much about him as what he wrote.

Deeper theological rejection of this court religion came with the Jansenistic piety of Port Royal, whose devotees were recommended by Hamon to close their eyes when they prayed in a beautiful church. Mére Angelique stripped the Port Royal chapel and said, 'I love all that is ugly, art is nothing but lies and vanity. Whosoever gives to the senses takes away from God.'

Here and down to the time of the Synod of Pistoia (1786) and for a long time afterward we see a concern for liturgy, for simplicity and a sense of mystery in worship, for popular participation, fatally compromised with the ancient recurrent divorce between flesh and spirit. Baroque at its best had celebrated their marriage, but the tendency to use baroque as a kind of theological saturation-bombing had at times led even reputable artists and their Church patrons into devout utilitarianism, sentimentality and the philistine brashness which superimposed a rococo apse on the Byzantine Sant' Apollinare Nuovo in Ravenna. This and many less spectacular outrages have been removed in our less creative but more critical age, though one of the worst obstinately survives — the late baroque choir loft in S Cecilia, Rome, which shuts off from public view Cavallini's masterly Last Judgement and even buries the lower half of it altogether.

Insistence on the more sober elements in the Renaissance

heritage had already been present in Italy in the work of Andrea Palladio of Vicenza, who built three or four of the most beautiful churches in Venice, full of subtle light and modelling, but whose name passed into architectural language through his serene country houses, whose influence was so great in England and America. It was from this and from French sources that the revival of church-building in England mainly derived, but even in the great German baroque city of Dresden, where the Lutheran Frauenkirche was built in the golden period of 1726-43, the use of baroque and rococo resources does not disguise but emphasises the difference of theological inspiration. For the reformer, mistrust of auxiliary mediation was a central point, the word held primacy — it was sufficient means given by God for a pure relationship with the one Mediator. Luxuriance of images was an attempt to cover poverty of preaching; they had no power to put man in touch with the transcendent. Speech is prophetic, because it is free, mobile, susceptible to correction.

This is the argument in its soberer form: in the more violent forms of which sectarian history has made us more conscious, it was inspired by the levelling, iconoclastic spirit of puritanism, with a hatred of court and ritual rooted in aversion from multiplicity, variety, sensuous attractiveness. One reason why Laud and his revival came to a tragic end is expressed by an observer at Oxford in 1636:

> the churches or chapels of all the colleges are much beautified, extraordinary cost bestowed on them; most of the nave glazed, richer glass for figures and painting I have not seen, which they had most from beyond the Seas. . ., excellent pictures, large and great church works of the best hands they could get. . .

Yet the moderate and humane spirit of Anglicanism survived the execution of Charles I, the most munificent of royal art-patrons, and manifested itself after the Fire of London in the genius of the amateur Wren with his inexhaustible variations on an idiomatic theme, in the English editions of

Roman work by the Roman-trained Gibbs and the frank baroque exuberance of Hawksmoor. Yet the theological difference remains. Baroque is often called 'theatrical', but in the Catholic world it is the opera-house that derives from the church, not vice-versa. A Wren church, and still more the Dresden Frauenkirche of George Bahr, were designed like theatres because they were designed for the hearing of the word. The same is true on a simpler scale of a building like the Wesley chapel in Bristol.

Rembrandt (1606-69) offers something of a bridge between the baroque illustrators and Calvinism, though he was a private genius whose profound biblical paintings owed nothing to ecclesiastical patronage. His earlier religious work exploits biblical drama in an extrovert, baroque way, but his later work, e.g. 'Woman taken in Adultery' (National Gallery), links him more, *mutatis mutandis*, with El Greco or Tintoretto.

One reason why Rembrandt's Bible painting is the highest art is its inclusiveness — it achieves intense seriousness without the puritan solemnity which walls off the sacred from the profane and puts theology always in Sunday clothes. What this means is best illustrated by looking at the interplay of religion and poetry in England. Reformed mistrust of the image and insistence on the word did not rule out poetry, and our religious poetry in the seventeenth century is a rich vein; yet puritan decorum contributed to the rupture of religious from secular interest which afflicted poetry and especially poetic drama. The authors of the medieval mysteries had possibly fused too readily the religious with the earthy, but Langland and Chaucer in their different ways show how criticism of life which is essentially theological gains force and maturity from a vast range of reference in both learned and popular experience. This power reaches its climax in the best Elizabethan and Jacobean drama, but also in the poetry of Donne and Herbert. A simple isolated example may be quoted, though it gives no idea of the rich texture into which religious and other sensibilities are woven; Marlowe's Renaissance scholar Faustus in his last speech, wanting to put off the dreadful end, quotes Horace's *O lente, lente currite noctis equi* — originally spoken by the pagan poet as he lay under the stars with his love. This command of dramatic intensification through irony depends on a range of reference and response which has spiritual affinities with the baroque. There has been a lot of sterile argument about 'Shakespeare's religion', but what cannot be argued about is that his poetry would have neither meaning nor impact apart from the rich Christian inheritance which he alludes to so rarely and obliquely but which forms the very texture of his imagery. In Donne and Herbert the religious interest is explicit enough, but the sharpness of perception, the easy fusion of disparate ideas and feelings, gives rich texture and carries theology into every corner of experience. At its worst this may convey an uneasy sense of getting the best of both worlds; yet Donne's 'tortured' verse, agonising over where truth lies, is in the end less self-defeating than the single-minded, proselytising solemnity of Milton's grand style.

In the classical Anglican theologians of the seventeenth century literary art powerfully reinforces argument, and we can feel their oneness with the poets. In France the relevance, in this sense, of art to theology was most startlingly demonstrated by Pascal — the brevity, tautness and precision by which he helped to lay the foundations of French prose made him a formidable opponent of the French establishment. But subsequently the balance of literary art was perhaps on the side of the more fundamental opponents of tradition — Hume, Voltaire, Rousseau.

If we accept Pevsner's limit of 1760 we can, from the vantage point of today, see a new world coming into being during the century preceding it. Behind the facade of Louis XIV's traditionalist absolutism in France, a scientific revolution was beginning as men often intended for the priesthood became bored with the traditional curriculum and turned to Descartes and scientific works. Science became socially smart, was popularised, and the popularisers turned it into a world-view which dominated the philosophers of the next century. Descartes, Kepler, Boyle, Newton were all Christians of various degrees of piety, but literary men drew from, or grafted on to, their work a scepticism derived from literary sources. Obstructive traditionalism made this easier — a divided, weak Christendom was failing to absorb a substantial new development in western thought. There was an appeal from the Churches and the universities to a growing middle-class, from which in France, for example, the greatest men of the age of Louis XIV came. The 'reason' after which the age came to be known was something very like the common sense of the man in the street — the 'sensible men' whose religion Deism claimed to be. It was by nature no friend of baroque art. Baroque was the end of the road for architecture and art as an integrated and living instrument of the Church. It had assimilated as much as was possible (and perhaps some that was not) of the classical Renaissance, but what was happening in the second half of the seventeenth century and on into the eighteenth was simply not being assimilated at all, yet was to make a radically new and perhaps ultimately alien world. The scientific revolution was to prove the central thing, but the enlargement of the known world, the growth of overseas trade, the industrial and agrarian revolution, utopian schemes for social reform, the replacement of religious wars by wars for trade, all went to make up a world in which Christianity lost the directing role, so that Catholicism, remaining chiefly conservative, and Protestantism, liberal-national or pietistic, existed within it, adapting themselves with varying success. This is a world in which the centre of gravity (for reasons other than artistic) shifts from the baroque regions to Britain, France and Holland.

The secularisation-process gathers momentum at a time when Christian theology is least equipped by temperament and resources to handle it. Bacon, whom the French, with that curious uncertainty which marks their bouts of Anglophilia, had made the patron saint of the enlightenment, said rather restrainedly of the scholastics that they had 'subtle and strong capacities, abundance of leisure and but small variety of reading.' Art since the sixteenth century had both demanded and manifested an enlargement of reading but not a growth of critical sense. The long struggle over the Jansenist appeal to Augustine already shook the theory of unchanging tradition, and the 'disinterested' history of the school of St Maur did so more thoroughly. Tension between the scholar and the conservative-in-power was beginning — less noisily than the clash with 'reason' and the enlightenment, but more important in the end perhaps for theology and art: conscious questioning of tradition came only from the 'enemies' who could be ruled out of court, but historical sense and placing would modify the notion of tradition from within.

The changes we can now see as radical were not obvious then or for long afterwards. No one in the eighteenth century would have thought of cutting themselves off from the Graeco-Roman inheritance and few from the Christian inheritance, even if they could have done so. Hence it is not surprising that those who set out in the spirit of the age to purge or simplify Christian art and those who looked for an iconography for the French revolution turned the clock back in the same way. Neo-classicism became the formula for both. The revolutionaries did rather better out of it.

The ambiguous Winckelmann, of whom it was written 'Moderation and form, simplicity and noble line, stillness of soul and gentleness of sensibility, these were the main tenets of his creed. His favourite symbol was crystal-clear water', could be taken on as Keeper of Antiquities at the Vatican, and his clammy influence obtrudes in Rome to this day, especially in St Peter's and the Vatican. The tombs and statues of Canova and Thorwaldsen look, beside those of Michelangelo and Bernini, as if they are intended for museums from the outset. If the best baroque churches had aimed at the illusion of heaven, the neo-classical achieved the reality of a mausoleum. Unlike the Renaissance, neo-classicism was a return not to a living spring but to a musty cupboard. It drained the blood out of Christian art and architecture but put nothing theological or artistic in. After all, the same designs served equally well for opera-houses, market halls, and even railway stations, where they were handled with more enthusiasm.

The fact is that we do not, after 1760, look to the visual arts for the strongest impulses expressing the spirit of the age — an age which yet differed from the past more radically than any other we have had to look at in this essay. The accomplished but rather chilly neo-classicism of David, a kind of official artist to the more virtuous, republican side of the French Revolution, hardly expresses the radical, visionary character of the changes and aspirations of the age. For this we must go to music like that of Beethoven or to literature. One aspect of the new spirit, the divinisation of nature (itself a consequence of the recession of Christianity from the spheres of creative thought and feeling), received expression in painting as well as poetry, not least in England, but visual artists show little of the social concern which was challenging theology and with which the Church was failing to make vital contact. Generous and heroic impulses like the passion for freedom which dominates, say, *Fidelio*, found little enough response in the arts the Church patronised. European churches were full of visual reminders of a view of life which the revolutionary idealism of Rousseau wished to replace utterly. Liberal optimism and the belief in progress, whether in its rational or apocalpytic forms, ended in disappointment in the sense that the French Revolution ended in violence and destruction and was followed by a conservative reaction, and there was no immediate achievement of a new social, economic or moral order. The conservative reaction, which formally was largely successful, was not a restoration of the state of things which had made baroque and rococo possible. When Fichte described belief in the hereafter as 'that lunacy according to which the whole of Christendom will assemble in a concert-hall perpetually to sing Hallelujah', he was not revealing a great discovery shared by large numbers of people, but he was pointing accurately to the crack which was opening between the old sensibility and the new. Imagination was to move away from the paths of theology. The baroque ceiling had opened a visual heaven which was nevertheless the opening from one reality on to another, which was its logical consummation. When romanticism sought in art a retreat from the intolerable realities of war or utilitarianism or the industrial revolution, there was no such logical transition but only an escape. If baroque art lent some plausibility to describing religion as the opium of the people, nineteenth-century art, or twentieth-century perhaps even more (we shall have to raise this question again), was much more certainly the opium of the aesthetic elite.

If this is read as a simple statement that nineteenth-century art, or 'romantic art', was 'not religious', it will of course look very implausible from some points of view. Those who are interested in arithmetic can perhaps show that more churches were built in industrially expanding countries, new or old, than in the great epochs of Christian art. But this only brings us back to Pevsner's dictum and its required explanation. It is more useful to begin by reflecting that the 'romantic movement', if we can use the phrase at all, was an extremely complex affair. Proust claimed that 'only the romantics know how to read classical works, because they read them as they were written, romantically.' However that may be, the whole idea of the reign of Reason with its appropriate *cult naturel* parodying Christianity, as portrayed in the famous etching, is solemnly romantic — a romantic optimism which led quite naturally to the no less solemnly romantic disillusion and despair of much nineteenth-century painting and poetry and perhaps to the less savoury features of the 'Romantic Agony'. Similarly, early attitudes to the scientific and industrial revolution were very romantically optimistic, and it took years of cruelty, oppression and perhaps irreparable damage to society and the environment before suspicion of the whole enterprise could have any practical effect.

This healthy suspicion is found on the whole (if one excepts the great English evangelicals) much earlier among artists and art-critics than theologians. A conservative-minded Church, on the defensive against great forces of change, tended to insist on the visible, historical, 'Roman' side of herself rather than the transcendent. She thus invited judgment by the very standards on which she was most vulnerable, those of the new optimistic age of progress. A Church seen *chiefly* as a vast historical institution can be seen as one that wears out, and is exposed to being superseded. There was a kind of 'salvation' which the world could be seen as bettering — the better world

107

of the industrial revolution was going to do more for man, by technology and the discipline of work, than Christian society had ever done.

It has often been pointed out that certain types of Protestant asceticism provided the industrial revolution with a moral impulse, extolling the gospel of work and thrift, discouraging extravagance, focussing life on the counting-house or the meeting-house, liable to consecrate greed. Once the more dreadful abuses of labour had been eliminated and dismissed as 'growing pains', prosperity and virtue were easily identified, and philistinism and drabness taken as their accompaniments. Organized religion too easily accepted the identification: protests came from novelists like Dickens, prophetic artists like Blake, satirical artists like Doré, critics like Ruskin. Theologians and Church leaders missed opportunities of alliance with them — though there are glimpses of the possibilities, as when Ruskin's social and artistic passion led him (by a route perhaps shorter than it seemed) from bigoted evangelicalism to friendship and collaboration with Manning, while F. D. Maurice, a professor of literature as well as of theology, drew the frowns of the establishment by his courageous response to the signs of the times.

Social involvement is not however characteristic of either theologian or artist in the nineteenth-century, though it was such an age of social change. The political enlistment of art typified by David in both his revolutionary and Bonapartist phases did not last: the real impact of the Revolution on art was to push to the furthest extreme ideas which had first appeared at the Renaissance but which under the *ancien regime* received limited practical expression. The romantic movement declared a war of liberation against academies, churches, courts, patrons. The idea of personal expression as unique, a law unto itself, entered on a long life, thought it was and has remained consistent with the dogmatism of coteries, cliques, and 'movements'. Johnson's confident appeal to 'the common reader' (as he understood the term) and his art-loving equivalent who could be found in the salons of Paris, an appeal founded on rapport which reflected an organic if limited society and world-view, lost its meaning. Religious commissions meant patronage and iconographical rules, and were not popular.

Romanticism had of course its religious side, but the theological pressure behind it was low. Disillusionment with the revolution, pessimism about the present, a feeling of inadequacy to cope with life as it is, moulds Chateaubriand's conception of the *Génie du Christianisme*, romantic aestheticism about Gothic cathedrals, Gregorian chant, liturgy, distant church bells, serving the turn of apologetics along with the eloquence of Bossuet and the brilliance of Pascal. The book had enormous vogue. More constructively, Ruskin looked back to Gothic as an art which harmoniously expressed the culture from which it sprang and contrasted the Gothic world favourably with that of liberal economics and *laissez-faire* capitalism. But it was a long and obscure way from this to filling industrial cities, growing rapidly in size and ugliness, with neo-Gothic churches, stations and insurance offices.

Down to about 1820, educated taste controlled the expansion of cities, particularly in domestic architecture. Romantic individualism and historical revivals played a limited and light-hearted part. But soon the scene was changing alarmingly. Architects were no longer looking for ways of expressing the character of their own age, but for means of getting away from it. Early French revival of interest in Gothic had been intelligent, impressed by its structural advantages, and this was never lacking in England, but was gradually swamped by obsession with detail — made easier by the development of such cheap, easily-worked materials as terra-cotta.

Historical crazes were not confined to Gothic but extended to exotic styles — Egyptian, Moorish, Persian, Chinese. Waves of fashion in architecture are more disastrous than in dress. Women sooner or later — usually sooner — throw their old clothes away. But when undiscriminating wealth and rapid expansion make historical fancies realisable in large-scale urban building, only modern war, exceptional civic courage or speculators' ruthlessness can get rid of the results. The first and last of these usually sweep away the good with the bad.

Intellectual vigour and originality was given visual embodiment in other things than the conventional fine arts — engineering for instance. The results were occasionally beautiful, but more often revealed no concern for man's sensibility. Yet the fact that a good railway viaduct sensitively placed can give pleasure where a fussy neo-Gothic church gives pain underlines the fact that nineteenth-century Christian art was out of gear with theology. Superficially the 'historical approach' dominated both art and theology (certainly in England where during the forty years after the Act of 1818 over six hundred churches were rushed up), but enriching understanding of Christian tradition by renewing scriptural, patristic and medieval scholarship is quite a different activity from building imitation Greek, Romanesque or early English churches, or colleges like thirteenth-century monasteries. The difference is greater in that the 'imitation' was often very partial or distorted, reflecting no accurate knowledge of what medieval buildings originally looked like and accepting the theological or aesthetic prejudices which had made the surviving ones look as they did in the nineteenth century.

Newman, who mistrusted eighteenth-century rationalism as well as scholasticism and was an advocate of the historical method, insisted that

> the heart is commonly reached not through reason
> but through the imagination, by means of direct
> impressions, by the testimony of facts and events, by
> history, by description ... Christianity is a history
> supernatural, and almost scenic: it tells us what its
> Author is by telling us what he has done.

This might almost be taken as a declaration that the arts are a necessary supplement to theology and a justification of the long history of Christian art (which however had most often flourished alongside a theology which expressed itself very differently). It can also be taken as expressing one side of nineteenth-century Romanticism. But such thoughts inspired no renewal of religious painting. Regeneration was taken as a programme by the Nazarener in Germany (1809 ff.) and less narrowly by the Pre-Raphaelites in England, but these were

110

programmes of deliberate historical recession, and their chief interest from our present point of view is that the Pre-Raphaelites in their brief period of brotherhood were reviled as crypto-Romanists.

The interests of painters were turned elsewhere, and the more painting renewed itself as the century went on, shaking off constricting labels and habits, the less it was concerned with Christian themes.

Several reasons can be suggested for this. Painters with non-academic methods and interests, technical or other, were not likely to get what ecclesiastical commissions there were. Where they were in protest against other aspects of the establishment besides academicism, these usually included the Church. Even Goya (1746-1828) a link with Tiepolo in one direction and Manet in the other, though he did some work for the Church and somehow managed to keep in with the Spanish establishment, spent much of his effort in satirising it. Yet Ruskin, who would have reckoned himself as trenchant a social critic as Goya and who linked his social criticism with his art criticism, is said to have thrown a set of Goya's 'Caprichos' on the fire, in an angry fit, in a London dealer's shop. There is the same incoherence between Morris's sound grasp of the relations of art and society with his consequent scathing criticism of the philistinism of his time, and his practical search for irretrievable past standards. The idea that industrialism and the machine were essentially enemies of good design was understandable in the Victorian age, but short-sighted.

Theologians who identified with this kind of criticism were really no better than those who joined the philistines and went to the repositories: in fact theology as a corrective in this age of crisis (which long out-lasted Victoria) was hardly active enough to be called a failure.

The treatment of the French Impressionists (who were not at all bellicose *avantgardistes*) by the Paris salons is the most notorious example of the rift between art and society. This irrational hostility has sometimes been given ideological shape: the impressionists, it is said, had a subjective and Heraclitan view of reality, they were materialist, positivist, sensualist, the 'climax of self-centred culture'. In reality they were tired of painting that looked like illustrations of expensive amateur theatricals (and in England brought official honours to artists like Alma-Tadema) and even their confessed hostility to the 'art of Museums' did not exclude proper relations to tradition, though it greatly narrowed their interest in traditional subjects.

A much better case could be made (even theologically) against the inbreeding aestheticism of the turn of the century which, whether thought of as 'decadent' or not, can hardly be seen as expressing a healthy relation of art and society.

PRESENT AND FUTURE

Some threads should be gathered before taking a rash look at the complications of the present century and attempting some general conclusions.

It cannot be simply taken for granted that the visual arts have any future in the Christian community, or even in the human community. It is no longer even a dogma that the Christian assembly needs a special building. A long list of reasons can be given why the importance of painting and sculpture should be shrinking especially in the religious sphere.

Yet there has never been an age when so much exact knowledge about the art of the past was so widely available, nor when architect and artist showed such vigour of experiment and had such variety of materials and techniques in which to show it. These facts considerably weaken the argument that our prejudices and enthusiasms may in the end go the same way as those of, say, the Victorians. We know more than they did. On the other hand, T. S. Eliot (one of the indisputably great Christian artists and critics of our time) has warned us that 'the less you know and like, the easier it is to frame aesthetic laws . . . We know too much and are convinced of too little.' In the arts the theologian, or at least the churchman, tends to know too little and be convinced of too much, though even here there are signs of gaining prudence.

If we assume that the artistic impulse will never be lost but at most transmuted in one way or another, and that the place of art in society will always be a question integral to social health (cf. p. 127), then the theologian will always be concerned about the arts. How?

The enormous weight of historical precedent directs attention first to 'religious' art, but this is not the only *possible* concern of the theologian. There are questions of 'taste' considered not as caprice or as the preserve of a coterie but as an index of the health of a society, which should interest them; as suggested earlier, the shrinkage of the

Church's role as patron and promoter has tended to expand her less assured role of external, and none too discerning, moral censor. There are also questions of the relation of art and society, a whole range of questions to which the modern theologian, in spite of his rapidly expanding interests, has contributed little. We may take these in order, but they are not really separable.

Religious art may concern the theologian either as a historical fact or as a fact of the present and future Christian life. If theology seeks to develop and better the expression of the content of faith through participation and reflection on that faith as experienced in the life of a community of faith (the definition is roughly John Macquarrie's), then it has been argued here that the historical inheritance of Christian art offers a vast and largely untapped source. There are reasons for this neglect, and consequences of it. Theology has often fallen into the danger of departmentalising itself too much. This has been combined with a too utilitarian and minimalist approach to ministry-training, in which real mental and affective needs are starved or supplied by a tacked-on 'spirituality' as jejune as the theology. This is not an exclusively Roman weakness, — a contributor to the Anglican *Soundings* wrote harshly:

> For decades, if not generations, Christian faith has lived in a state of imaginative impoverishment. How should it not? The Church has lived in almost total isolation from the arts. Academic theology has lived on its own fat. The supply of fat is running out.[1]

Bryan Wilson, the sociologist of religion, echoes the metaphor in reverse when he speaks of religious arts being 'steadily emaciated' in modern times.

If we have realised belatedly that our artistic inheritance is not there to be copied, we still need to realise fully that it is a source of enrichment of Christian life, which will work only if the theologian is tapping it. We can now speak of the life of faith as experienced without being charged with 'empiricism'

---

(1) H. Root in A.R. Vidler (ed.), *Soundings* (Cambridge University Press 1962).

or 'subjectivism'. The shared function of theology and art can be seen as one of illustrating this experience if we understand illustration richly enough. Between them they should *make sense* of it, for the *whole* man. By contrast, there is poverty, as well as historical error, in the pragmatic view of religious art which sees its symbolism as a mere expedient to impress on untutored minds truths that the developed intelligence can turn into clear and distinct ideas. This is to take one of two equally important modes of perception and debase it to the level of a mere means to the other.

A true conception of our relation to the art of the past already contributes to examining the present and future prospects of religious art. These strike many at first sight as bleak. Though a vast amount of both historical and contemporary art is more generally accessible, it is argued that the influence and interest of the visual arts is contracting, not expanding. This however is not a problem peculiar to religious art. More relevant perhaps is the argument (itself doubtful) that first the growth of literacy and the availability of print, then the enormous expansion of the performing arts, successively through cinema, radio and television, have drawn away attention from the fine arts, since the fine arts, in many countries were most generally accessible in church, and at least reminded practising Christians of a great past — a reminder usually sharpened by the additional presence of commercial religious art. Since the art forms created by the technological age reflect mainly the estrangement of Church and artist, and far fewer people go to historic churches to worship, the impression is strengthened that to see a link between the satisfactions of art and those of religion is an anachronism, or at best productive of a vague uplift. An age saturated with 'realistic' images, technically multiplied, seems also to be an age in which the painter and sculptor have retreated into private worlds; esotericism, cliquishness, sectarianism abound (the present century counts more movements, manifestos and styles — though the last word is not popular — than all others put together); generally speaking, modern art is 'abstract' (blessed word), personalist, subjective in origins and arbitrary

115

in conventions, not aspiring to monumentality or public ritual function.

To these arguments must be added those of some phases of liturgical reform. The needs of liturgy have sometimes confusedly been thought a sufficient *aesthetic* criterion — this a reflection of the general 'functionalist' theory which rather bleakly affected architecture for a time. This was a healthy reaction against fussy historicism but was carried too far in a puritan spirit. Liturgical needs hardly affect more than the horizontal placing of elements in a church, and the total articulation of space and volume remains, as it always has been, a stimulus to the architect's skill and insight.

The reformist inclined at first to banish all decoration from churches, sometimes in the doctrinaire spirit of Constructivism or Le Corbusier's 'purism', sometimes out of uncertainty about how to treat new forms, sometimes in healthy if extreme reaction to the sentimental clutter of the immediate past (which in any case continued in conservative practice, sometimes with a few crude gestures towards the 'modern').

This rather dreary picture is by now one-sided and misleading. It is half-a-century since the pioneer 'modern' church of Notre Dame de Raincy near Paris was built by the Perret brothers. It already shows something of the chief virtues of reinforced concrete structure — lightness, cheapness and flexibility, while elegance of line and free use of glass help to disguise its defects: cheerlessness, unpleasing texture and unfinished look. But the virtues were not likely to appeal to those with rigid habits of thought about 'what a church should look like', and the new manner made very unequal strides in different countries. Down to the second World War of course the need for new churches was mainly restricted to expanding suburbs. The bombers then provided on a European scale an opportunity similar to that given to Wren by the Great Fire. Thus in the last quarter of a century a kind of church building which represents possibly history's biggest complex of innovations in structural principle, materials and design, has been able to mature with a rapidity perhaps unparalleled since the early Gothic. Not everywhere of course — down to the day before yesterday churchmen, in England especially, who could no longer afford historical fancies or even those who had developed a liturgical conscience still preferred to entrust their commissions to builders with plenty of commercial bricks and no fancy ideas. The fact that we now have in England two modern Roman Catholic cathedrals is significant — if you accept that cathedrals should still be built (cf. below, p. 122).

The combination of post-war opportunity arising from reconstruction needs, bold architectural invention and serious theological thinking about the possibilities of church art and architecture has been strongest and most fertile in Germany, and it is interesting that this has gone with loving and brilliant renovation of the baroque and rococo masterpieces of Bavaria, Baden-Wurtemburg and Franconia. By contrast the brilliant Italian moderns, who are second to none, have been given little ecclesiastical scope, and the abbey of Monte Cassino has been laboriously rebuilt at astronomical expense in its original mediocre baroque — this in the country of Nervi and Ponti. But Nervi *has* built the new audience chamber in the Vatican.

The spectacular recent extension of technical resources and of materials for both structure and revetment made possible (though not of course certain) an imaginative renewal and expansion which has some parallel in a new and vigorous theology of worship. This involves the clearing away of some stylistic and iconographic rubble. Advances in scriptural and historical scholarship must result in the pruning of iconography, though something more is needed for its renewal.

The layman sees the greatest obstacle, or the greatest gulf between history and present practice in what he rather vaguely understands as 'abstract' or 'non-figurative' art, meaning primarily an object which he cannot identify by referring to nature, experience, literature (Bible, hagiography or whatever), whether directly or through the medium of a code of symbols or an allegorical scheme. A first-stage answer here of course is that such 'abstract' work is not peculiar to twentieth-century art, but as old as religious art itself: geometrical forms played a large part in Byzantine art, in Anglo-Saxon and Celtic Gospel-books (cf. pp. 44-45), in Romanesque capitals and reliefs; in cosmatesque work, in stained glass. The Cistercian reaction strongly favoured it. Facades like S Miniato or some in the Pisan style depend entirely on it. Figurative art too works by abstraction — even the most 'realistic' or 'photographic' painting, if it is any good, selects, emphasises and even distorts. In fact this is what the spectator responds to.

But it is one thing to have images which are referable to reality, or can simply be accepted as pleasing patterns, and quite another to be confronted by an image of which one can make absolutely nothing or for which one may even feel some revulsion, and have it entitled 'Eucharist' or 'Pentecost' or what-not. This raises a number of legitimate questions in the lay mind. Can a private or esoteric artistic language be properly used in a place of public worship? Or if it is claimed that such a language is worth being made public (because it will increase our penetration of the mystery of faith), where lies the duty of mediation? Should such an artistic language be one in which the theologian has a creative part?

We are familiar since the romantic age with the notion of the artist as a lonely, alienated figure, starving in a garret (except that nowadays he is more likely to be lonely, alienated and comfortably off). The present age presents, according to Rahner at least, the more startling figure of the lonely, alienated theologian, who 'cannot regard himself as a member of a team of workers constructing a single building according to a single plan with which all are familiar' (the metaphor chosen is interesting). Today the *rudis* is not merely the uneducated — in an age of daunting specialisation the problem of finding adequate grounds for an act of faith affects almost everybody. Rahner seems to call for a re-orientation towards mystery, 'an original experience of the Spirit to which theology must be related and which it must serve'. One is reminded of Eliot's description of poetry as a 'raid on the inarticulate': perhaps the theologian and the artist may be brought together as fellow-strugglers rather than in a master-pupil relationship or one of censor and censored, or one of official and self-assured professional to rather dangerous amateur. It has been suggested earlier (p. 63) that the medievals, understanding the

118

needs of the full man, understood that art was not a poor substitute for theology but a complement to it. We may rediscover the same truth under different pressures.

The thesis advanced by Harvey Cox (a theologian from a strongly Protestant background) in his *Feast of Fools*, that 'in a success- and money-orientated society we need a re-birth of patently unproductive festivity and expressive celebration', has implications for theology and the arts. Science itself has advanced by brilliant imagination, but the world of applied sciences, the dizzily changing world of science-for-profit, is weakening the imagination by which alone we might adapt to bewildering change. We live, says Cox, in a desperately harried age, which combines an almost Savonarola-like rejection of its past with cynicism about its future. Much artistic practice and *avant-garde* theology exemplifies the neurotic immolation of the past, of which Cox speaks, though one can hardly simply ignore the opposite phenomena, the passionate and brilliant dedication to art history and the renewed interest in, for example, all forms of baroque art which arguably of all historic styles most embodies what Cox means by festivity and fantasy. However that may be, Cox rightly asks why Christianity does not fulfil what might seem its natural function, 'to assist contemporary society to put aside its fatal contempt for the past'. His answer is worth quoting in full:

> The reason is that in Christianity itself today the mix is badly distorted, with a bias not toward the present or the future but toward the past. To many observers, Christianity today personifies contempt for the flesh, a suspicion of sexuality, a distrust of present experience. Furthermore, Christianity seems to harbour a deep fear of the future and to live on a compulsive attachment to bygone ages. So long as this condition persists, no Christian corrective to our culture's contempt for the past will be possible.
>
> The modern sensibility is correct in warning us that the past should have no favoured status. It was not better, more virtuous, or closer to God. But in its crusade against the past, the modern sensibility has fallen into the snares of uncritical presentism and

futurism, snares an alert theology might have helped
it avoid. But theology is in no position to remove the
mote from our culture's eye until it removes the
beam from its own.(2)

'Alert' is an interesting choice of word. Theology is missing
something, and what it is missing is the other-than-intellectual
dimension of some of its problems. There are few people from
whose lives God is missing merely because they have not
solved, or have solved negatively, an intellectual problem.
Equally few are likely to find him again by following an argument. It has been said that the history of Catholic Christianity
is one vast effort to keep the distant God near at hand; but
today our world has become neutral, a framework for research, a chain of facts to be investigated. It is no longer
charged with another reality: it stimulates curiosity but not
reverence.

This is not fair to all scientists, and I would say that in the
Catholic world reverence has rather been distorted and
swamped; it appears exaggeratedly in many churchy contexts,
but in a wider range of matters we accept the standards of a
world which, as a predecessor of Cox's at Harvard, Samuel
Miller, wrote, 'has for three hundred years been stripping
nature of its religious implications'. 'Today's world,' he adds,
'provides us with no resonance, no rapport with nature; it is a
non-nature world, a technique world,' and 'technique is a way
of getting results without involving the self'.(3) The frightening consequences of this can be glimpsed by talking to any
well-informed scientist interested in environment problems.
But a small number of theologians are even interested.

One thing the sculptor of Southwell chapter-house has in
common with Henry Moore (to take at random two superficially disparate examples) is this resonance and rapport with

_____

(2) H. Cox, *Feast of Fools* (Harvard University Press 1970),
pp. 42-3.

(3) Samuel Miller, in *Anglican Theological Review*, January
1968, pp. 78-9.

120

nature, whether leaf, flower or stone. By contrast, in spite of multiplying departments of theology in universities (American ones at least) and the pullulation of 'theologies of' this and that, many would agree with Cox, echoing Robert Bellah, that 'the theologian must widen his sights'. This means widening not abdicating a critical function, but a critical function which is not confused with a negative type of censorship from outside, confusing the theologically interesting with the churchy. The theologian who assumes that a film called (say) *The Ten Commandments* is necessarily more interesting to him than one called (say) *Zabriskie Point* or *Blow-up* may be an extreme case of obtuseness, but he is not as rare as he should be.

Harvey Cox in another of his writings contrasts our Promethean attitude (through our scientists) to nature and to space with our inert fatalism about the mindless rash of city growth. Rational thinking and resolve about cities is he says 'a religious undertaking before any temple is constructed'. History is with him. From the oriental and Hellenistic temple-cities, where religious symbolism was joined to great technological efficiency, down to the founding of Constantinople (whose solemn ritual character is described by Gibbon), to the medieval cities of western Europe, the planning of cities was thought important enough to be religious. Sometimes (as in the puritan foundations in America) religion imposed too much 'integration'. The sprawl of nineteenth-century industrial slums and twentieth-century suburbia, the monuments of 'decent godless people', as the poet has it, remains a testimony to the absence of mind of Churches who were still concerned with *terra cotta* twiddles and inferior stained glass.

Today there are plenty of signs both in the planning of new cities and in the clearing and renewal of old ones, of a new sensitivity and ambition to create human environments, though the contrary forces are still powerful. Brave humanising efforts can exist side by side with the worst excesses of speculative building. One of the Churches' most serious duties is to throw their weight on the side of the angels in this. A Church which cannot keep us above barbarism here is less likely than ever to be very convincing about the hereafter.

When we look again at the Churches' closest contribution to today's man-made environment, that is at religious building, we find, along with further rapid advances in techniques, theological thinking which goes far beyond consideration of mere liturgical propriety. Not only is historical revivalism rejected, but any kind of monumentalism. This position is reached from various directions. Perhaps, the most respectable argument today is also the oldest — the sumptuary one (cf. Ch. 7, p. 81). Historically it did not get off to a good start. Leaving aside the Old Testament, it was used first by Christ's disciples on one unhappy occasion (Mt 26. 8-11), but, as suggested earlier, it has recurred more impressively in history, and in an age in which we fail to prevent people starving it is easy to give grave scandal by stupid expenditure. The fact remains that it is not the people who spend least on building or embellishing churches who do most to relieve want: the two forms of expenditure tend to go together, as with the Germans. Nor of course is quality equated with expensiveness.

A related argument stresses the contrast between the Church's position and conception of herself from, say, Constantine to the French Revolution — the age of successive monumental styles — and the position and conception of herself which she has, somewhat belatedly, reached today, when the 'servant-Church' is the most acceptable cliché. A servant-Church should not put up prestige buildings: magniloquence and opulence should be rejected, modesty and homeliness sought after. This is a broader argument than the old puritan one of early liturgical revival (which was often consistent with reckless expenditure), especially when it goes further and claims that decorative overstatement, a too talkative and obtrusive symbolism, may hamper and not mediate 'encounter'. The risk with this kind of argument, with all its weight, is of erecting it into a dogma which takes no account of artistic criteria. Such disturbance and distraction may be due to failure of artistic organisation and harmony, and can be far worse in a clinical modern church than in a masterpiece by Zimmermann.

The spire is often fastened on as an easy example of an

expensive anachronism, which is true enough provided we remember what the medieval symbolism of a spire was, and so realise that putting one between two high office blocks makes nonsense of even its historic significance. (Nor does the fact that you don't build spires in megalopolis or suburbia detract from the enduring significance of the spires of Chartres or a Northamptonshire village; the fact that there are some people in Chartres and Northamptonshire to whom they do not 'speak' is another question altogether.)

The current 'theology of secularisation' has its effect in developing the anti-monumental argument still further, sometimes to extremes. There is a relation of course with the servant-Church argument. The Anglican J. G. Davies puts it well:

The Church exists, not for itself, but for others; it should therefore be an agent of reconciliation and liberation; it should concern itself with humanisation; it should seek to meet the needs of men in the totality of their physical and spiritual existence. It should therefore plan its buildings in terms of the human needs of that sector of society within which it is serving, irrespective of whether or not those in need call themselves Christian. This is to say that we should plan multipurpose buildings, the functions of which are determined not primarily by the restricted liturgical needs of a Christian group. The plan I am advocating, and it is capable of infinite variety, is one that embraces both sacred and secular within a single volume; one which neither shuts off the liturgy from the world nor the world from the liturgy. I am able to say this as a Christian, because I believe that in Christ sacred and secular are united; for me therefore, as for the early Christian community, there can be no specially holy places; it is in and through the world of man, the secular, that we encounter the divine. I cannot carve up life into distinct spheres, one sacred, one secular, and I cannot therefore argue for sacred buildings as distinct from secular ones. Such a view I would suggest is that of the New Testament, of the early Christian Church and of all the great Reformers.[4]

(4) J.G. Davies, in 'Revolution Place and Symbol', R.L. Hunt (ed.), *International Congress on Religious Architecture and Visual Arts* (New York, 1967).

There are many assumptions here, and perhaps something of the ambivalence which von Weizsacker, one of its originators, saw in the idea of secularisation.

I have already suggested that there are special reasons why a scholarly recourse to the New Testament and the early Church (or to any historical period) can be wholly fruitful for theology and wholly misleading for church architecture, which was impossible for Christians in those periods. The fact that we cannot carve up life into the sacred and the secular (it was not the high tradition of art that did this) and that we encounter the divine through the world of man, has historically been seen as justifying the full use of the resources of the world of man in multiplying means of encounter with God — in other words as justifying Christian art and architecture. It may well justify much more sensitive planning and citing of churches in relation to the community's needs rather than narrowly liturgical or worse sectarian principles. I should hesitate to see it as justifying ambitious 'multipurpose' schemes (at least under the Church's initative and management) of the sort which might suggest religion was being diluted to the pursuit of social aims which secular agencies achieve better. I see a stronger argument against the 'monumentality' which is equated with mere size and expense in the fact that today most of it goes into sheltering and proclaiming enterprises which no theological acrobatics could see as Christian. 'Centre Point', for instance. It is said that we are Christians not by inheritance but by commitment — but the antithesis is clearly fallacious; inheritance underlies and enhances the commitment of a man who possesses his past. But the 'monumental' has nothing to do, etymologically or otherwise, with size, expense or ostentation. Some of the greatest Christian monuments are tiny, rough things in inaccessible mountain valleys. A monument links our hearts and minds with our origins. It makes us remember, like the anamnesis of the liturgy; today's and tomorrow's Church will be 'monumental' so far as it helps not hinders anamnesis; anamnesis sometimes involves going out to the ambiguous world and sometimes recoiling from it.

In its extreme form the secularisation-argument sees no case for external manifestation of a church at all. 'There is no 'sacred place' — the building becomes the house of God only through the congregation', is a view compatible surely with only a very 'low' view of eucharistic presence. The proper rehabilitation of the Christian assembly and of the flexibility and dynamism restored to liturgical and architectural thinking hardly commits us to this extreme.

A pagan concept of the Holy place, which housed the often repulsive statue of the god and was a place of terror, has never been taken into Christianity. The church has been home, where the believer encountered the sacramental presence of his God and found forgiveness, refuge, peace. The community-conscious theologizing of our day, telling us in its constant, confident, rather suffocating way what we need and ought to want in church, overstresses the need for intimacy and club-biness and forgets the equal need for anonymity and silence. Architects often sense this better than theologians. But then it will be a frightening day when commissions of earnest litur-gists deliver prescriptions to architects like doctors to chemists.

Secularisation-theology has its say about the commissioning of works of art for the Church. 'Modern' artists who are now established masters, like Matisse (in his last days), Rouault, Leger, Chagall, Sutherland and Manzù, have done famous church commissions, and the Vatican collection has just now been augmented by filling the Borgia apartments with modern works. But fearless critics have been known to class all this rather airily with the mule — without pride of ancestry or hope of posterity: an American Jesuit told an international congress in New York a few years ago: 'However it may have worked in past ages, to paint on commission is entirely alien to a working method that is dedicated to the uncompromising pursuit of an interior vision.' I cannot see how this makes any more sense today than it ever did, unless we accept a vastly more comprehensive meaning of 'commissioning' than the common one of 'ordering and paying for'. Nearly all artists are commissioned in this sense. The question whether an artist pursues an interior vision is of no interest apart from that of whether he catches and *communicates* it — the thing is visual and must at least suggest to the sympathetic view that the pursuit is getting somewhere; otherwise we depend for our assurance about the pursuit on the artist's word, or on that of those who for very various reasons may not wish to contradict him. But of course we shall have no more assurance about the pursuit or the capture because a theologian (or a canon-lawyer) gives advance instructions or subsequent vetoes. Sympathetic discussion between theologians and artists both of whom understand the total problem is more likely to bring light. Le Corbusier, for example, believes that art is for the chosen few, though his own best known work (to my mind brilliant and opening up the vast plastic possibilities of modern building) is a popular country pilgrimage-chapel. Lord Clark has written: 'an image achieves the concentration, clarity and rhythmic energy that makes it memorable only when it illustrates or confirms what a minority believes to be an important truth.' It may then become popular, as with Franciscan-inspired art or baroque, but the chances of this are much reduced today. The latest dizzy advances in the spread and range of technological change are exposing the fallacy inherited from an earlier phase of industrialism, that 'mass-culture' creates a dead uniformity of taste and desires. The spread in quantity and variety of higher education breaks up standardisation and offers a range of choices which widens steadily, though not fast enough for discontented students. Even advertising, that accurate weather-vane, increasingly shifts the weight of its appeal from popularity to individual or discriminating-minority appeal. Tofler even argues that the trend of the future will be to replace one kind of cramping of freedom — mass-uniformity — with another kind, which he calls over-choice — 'a crazy-quilt pattern of evanescent life-styles'. Some would see this even in some recent developments of theology; it is hard to avoid seeing it in the arts, where the dizzy succession of experimental modes assimilates artefacts more and more to the disposable goods of commerce and drains the term masterpiece (still much used in newspaper

126

puffing) of all meaning. It may even be that the traditional work of art will finally give way to the 'happening'. Huxley's *Brave New World* has already been left far behind the facts.

The history of art, long dominated by religion, has given us a strong bias towards sacramentalising it (cf. p. 60). We are always expecting the work to point beyond itself — to 'say' something which, in proportion to the work's greatness, transcends the arrangement of pigment, the shaping of stone, the articulation of space, the manipulation of light. Obviously the sacramental character has been achieved more easily when beliefs have been given a generally recognized and acceptable symbolic form — in mythology or in Christian iconography. A successful symbol (p. 63) expresses something too complex, or too intense, or too remote, or too 'spiritual' for rational expression.

This kind of expectation merely irritates the more advanced modern, who sees the work as simply there — the arrangement, the shaping, the phenomenology is all. Against this, such a historically-minded critic as Lord Clark will lay it down as a *law* that 'a healthy and vital relationship exists between art and society when the majority feel that art is absolutely necessary to them, to confirm their beliefs, to inform them about matters of lasting importance and to make the invisible visible' (aims which might almost pass as those of theology) and adds that 'no great social arts can be based on material values or physical sensations alone'. The theologian may easily accept this so eagerly as to overlook the problems it raises.

Theologians today accept that (in the words of a principle fruitfully agreed on as a basis for Anglican-Roman Catholic dialogue) 'revealed truth is given in holy Scripture and formulated in dogmatic definitions through thought-forms and language which are historically conditioned'. Some would apply this to religious visual symbolism, and say we should fashion (or 'develop' to use a theologians' favourite escapeword) a set of symbols adapted to the present age. But you cannot produce for the fine arts a new 'set of symbols' as you could fit a new lock and key after a burglary. It is perhaps in the performing arts where involvement is so much more wide-

127

spread, especially among the young, that a confused recognition of Lord Clark's 'law' is developing and bringing about promising new lines of exploration. But there is a hard furrow to plough, as witness the fact that, just before I wrote this page, while *Jesus Christ Superstar* was being done in Rome, some hard-liners managed to arrange a Mass of reparation against it — a day or two before Paul VI said how much he enjoyed it. It matters little whether it is in the cinema, the studio, the theatre, the dance hall or in the painter's or sculptor's shop and the builder's yard that the artist pursues his vision, his raid on the inarticulate, if so be he recaptures what has too long been the scientist's monopoly, the confidence of success which comes from knowing that everybody needs him. There are still some things for which technology has provided no standards of measurement, nor is there any good reason to suppose it will. Whatever label you use to classify them, they are things which unite artist and theologian in one concern. And in the end it is a concern for man.

GLOSSARY

p. 22	*naos*	inner shrine chamber of a Greek temple
p. 27	*orans*	praying figure
p. 29	*hypogea*	underground burial chambers
p. 33	*chlamys*	kind of cloak or tunic
p. 34	*iconostasis* . .	screen covered with sacred images shutting off sanctuary from body of Orthodox church
p. 36	*memoriae*) *martyria*) ˙ ˙	Shrine at which celebration of anniversary of martyrs takes place (may or may not enshrine remains)
p. 36	*cemeteriales* .	basilicae built on burial site of saint
p. 36	*confessio* . . .	crypt-like opening under high altar (at crossing) marking point of patron saint's burial.
p. 37	*traditio legis* .	handing over of books of law
p. 40	*basileia*	kingship
p. 35	*pantocrator* .	ruler of all things
p. 35	*theotokos* . .	Mother of God
p. 68	*maniera greca*	greek manner
p. 72	*ascesis*	Disciplined moral/mystical exercise in pursuit of perfection
p. 74	*badia*	abbey
p.118	*rudis*	untutored person

129

SELECT READING LIST

The literature of theological reflection on the arts is modest in the extreme but that of art history and criticism is vast and constantly increasing. It includes extensive many-volume surveys such as the Pelican History of Art, which I have not bothered to mention here. Nor, with one exception, do I mention works in languages other than English if they have not, as far as I know, been translated. Where I have quoted Latin or Italian source-books I have made my own translations or paraphrases. The books listed are chosen because I have found them helpful to my theme or because in one way or another they bear on it and because they are reasonably accessible.

For readers of Italian, a most remarkable modestly priced series is the *"Classici dell'Arte"* published by Rizzoli in Milan, which devotes a volume to each of some eighty painters. Besides most admirable colour reproductions, each volume includes an anthology of critical writing from the painter's day to the present, a bibliography and exhaustive analytical notes on technique, iconography, attributions etc.

GENERAL

The Social History of Art (2 vol)		London 1951
	A.Hauser (trans.)	
The Meaning of Art	H.Read	London 1931
Purpose and Admiration	J.E.Barton	London 1932
The Nude	K.Clark	London 1956
The Voices of Silence	A.Malraux (trans.)	London 1974
Selected Essays	T.S.Eliot	London 1951
Choir of Muses	E.Gilson (trans.)	London 1953
The Intellectual History of Europe		London 1953
	F.Heer (trans.)	
Soundings	ed. A.R. Vidler	London 1966
Religion in Secular Society	B.R.Wilson	London 1966
The Feast of Fools	H.Cox	Harvard 1969
Signs and Symbols of Christian Art		New York 1954
	G.Ferguson	

Encyclopaedia of Themes and Subjects in Painting	H.Daniel & J.Berger	London 1971
Saints and their Emblems in British Churches	R.L.P.Milburn	Oxford 1957
Civilisation	Lord Clark	London 1969

Of the many general handbooks on architectural history Banister Fletcher still provides the most encyclopaedic collection of drawings and photographs, though the latter are rather old-fashioned and Sir. N. Pevsner still leads the field for unaffected good sense and perception, not least in religious matters. The Dictionary of Art and Artists by P & L Murray is an excellent reference book, especially in the larger illustrated form, London 1965.

CHAPTER 2

The Greek Experience	C.M.Bowra	London 1957
Greek Art	Gisela Richter	London 1959
The Beginnings of Christian Art	D.Talbot Rice	London 1957
The Beginnings of Christian Art	A.Grabar (trans.)	London 1967
Early Christian Art	W.F.Vollbach	London 1961
Atlas of the Early Christian World	F.Van der Meer & C.Mohrmann	London 1958

CHAPTER 3

Byzantine Architecture and Decoration	J.A.Hamilton	London 1933
Byzantine Art	D.Talbot Rice	London 1935
Byzantine Legacy	C.Stewart	London 1947
Byzantine Aesthetics	G.Mathew	London 1963
Sailing to Byzantium	O.Lancaster	London 1969

CHAPTER 4

The Wandering Scholars	H.Waddell	London 1927
Medieval Culture	C.H.Haskins	Oxford 1929
The Making of Europe	Christopher Dawson	London 1932
Religion and Culture	Christopher Dawson	London 1948

Religion and the Rise of Western Culture	C.Dawson	London 1950
Medieval Essays	Christopher Dawson	London 1953
Western Society and the Church in the Middle Ages	R.W.Southern	London 1970

CHAPTER 5

Fioretti of St. Francis	T.Okey (trans.)	London 1910
Mont. S.Michel and Chartres	H.Adams	London 1914
The Waning of the Middle Ages	J.Huizinger	London 1924
The Vision of Piers Plowman	W.Langland	London 1935
The Mystical Theology of St. Bernard	E.Gilson	London 1940
The Master Builders	J.Harvey	London 1950
The Gothic World	J.Harvey	London 1950
Gothic Art and Scholasticism	E.Panofsky	London 1957
The Gothic Image	Émile Mâle	London 1961
Art and Scholasticism	J.Maritain	London 1930

CHAPTER 6

Leonardo da Vinci	K.Clark	Cambridge 1939
Michelangelo	Michele Saponoro	London 1950
The Civilization of the Renaissance in Italy	J.Burckhardt (trans.)	London 1944
Piero della Francesca	K.Clark	London 1951
The Penguin Book of the Renaissance		London 1964
	J.H.Plumb	
Renaissance & Renascences in Western Art		
	E.Panofsky	London 1965
Palladio	J.S.Ackerman	London 1966
The Florentine Renaissance)	V.Cronin	London 1967
The Flowering of the Renaissance)		London 1969
Symbolic Images	E.H.Gombrich	London 1972
Tradition and Innovation in Renaissance Italy	Peter Burke	London 1974
Patrons and Artists in the Italian Renaissance	ed. D.S.Chambers	London 1970

CHAPTER 7

Southern Baroque Art.	Osbert Sitwell	London 1924
Tintoretto	Hans Tietze	London 1948

Patrons and Painters	Francis Haskell	London 1963
Renaissance and Baroque	Heinrich Wolfflin	London 1964
Bernini	Howard Hibberd	London 1965
St. Peter's	James Lees-Milne	London 1967
The Baroque	Germain Bazin. (trans.)	London 1968

CHAPTER 8

The Gothic Revival	K.Clark	London 1928
On Neo Classicism	Mario Praz (trans.)	London 1969
Architecture in the Age of Reason		
	E.Kaufmann.	Cambridge, Mass. 1955
Neo-Classicism: Style and Motif	H.Hawley	Cleveland 1964

CHAPTER 9

Towards Modern Art.	L.Goldscheider	London 1951
Contemporary Church Art	A.Henze & T.Filthaut	
	Eng.(trans.)	New York 1956
Revolution, Place and Symbol	ed. R.L.Hunt	New York 1967
The New Architecture of Europe		London 1962
	G.E.Kidder Smith